I0202242

BREAK FORTH

Becoming a Success Story

Apostle David Philemon

Royal Diadem Publishing Inc.

Dedication

To everyone who has ever dared to dream of a better life. This book is dedicated to you – the brave, the resilient, and the determined. May these pages inspire you to unlock your full potential, overcome obstacles, and become the success story you were meant to be. May your journey be filled with hope, faith, and the courage to pursue your passions. May your success story inspire others and ignite a ripple effect of positivity and transformation. Apostle Dr. David Philemon

.

CONTENTS

ACKNOWLEDGMENT

I am deeply grateful to the individuals who have supported me on this journey.

To my family, whose unwavering love and encouragement have been my rock – thank you for believing in me.

To my friends, who have offered valuable feedback, guidance, and prayers – your contributions have enriched this book immensely.

To my mentors, who have shared their wisdom, expertise, and experience – your influence has shaped me into who I am today.

To my editors, designers, and publishing team – your professionalism and dedication have brought this book to life.

And to those who have shared their success stories with me – your testimonies have inspired me to write this book. Thank you for being part of my success story. I am honored to share this journey with you.

Apostle Dr. David Philemon

INTRODUCTION

The Essence Of Success

S uccess is a journey, not a destination.
We are on a unique path, filled with challenges, opportunities, and lessons that shape who we are meant to become.

This book aims to guide you on that journey, helping you unlock the potential that lies within you.

As we go through life, we often encounter obstacles that may seem impossible.

However, it's essential to recognize that these challenges are not meant to hinder us; they are stepping stones that lead us to more significant achievements.

This book will examine success principles rooted in faith, purpose, and personal growth.

We will discover how to define success beyond societal expectations, emphasizing the importance of aligning with God's purpose for our lives.
"For we are God's handiwork, created in Christ Jesus to do good works, which God prepared in advance for us to do." (Ephesians 2:10, NIV)
You may ask yourself, "What does it truly mean to be successful?"

Success is not merely measured by material wealth or social status. It is about commanding good succession results, building healthy relationships, and nurturing a fulfilling life that brings joy and satisfaction.

Success is the ability to solve problems and bring about positive change in your life and the lives of others.

It is a personal journey of growth and development, where each day presents an opportunity to improve, learn, and thrive.
This book will give you actionable insights and spiritual principles to empower you to embrace your unique journey.

We will look into topics such as the significance of discipline, the value of relationships, and the necessity of a clear sense of destiny. Each chapter will provide practical steps to help you overcome challenges and celebrate victories, no matter how small.

As we begin this learning journey together, I encourage you to keep an open heart and mind.
Allow the words within these pages to inspire you to take action and pursue the extraordinary life God designed for you.

"For I know the plans I have for you," declares the Lord, "plans to prosper you and not to harm you, plans to give you hope and a future." (Jeremiah 29:11, NIV)

Remember, you were not created by chance; you are a success story waiting to unfold.
Let's begin this journey toward becoming the success story you were destined to be.

CHAPTER ONE

DEFINING SUCCESS – REDISCOVERING THE TRUE MEANING

Although everyone can relate to success, what success means to each of us varies considerably based on our experiences, goals, and beliefs.

Many people mistake success for achievement, fame, or wealth, yet these definitions frequently fail to capture its essence.

As the Bible reminds us, *"For we are God's handiwork, created in Christ Jesus to do good works, which God prepared in advance for us to do."* (Ephesians 2:10, NIV)

This verse emphasizes that success is defined by living a life following our divine purpose, not only by results from outward measurement.

Success As A Personal Journey

To truly define success, we must first acknowledge that it is inherently personal. What may be deemed successful for one individual might not hold the same weight for another.

For some, success could be reaching the pinnacle of their career, while for others, it might mean achieving a work-life balance that allows them to spend more time with family. The key is recognizing that success is not a one-size-fits-all concept.

The Bible encourages us, *"For we are God's handiwork, created in Christ Jesus to do good works, which God prepared in advance for us to do."* (Ephesians 2:10, NIV)

In our pursuit of success, we must reflect on our values, goals, and what truly brings us fulfillment.
Are we chasing societal standards of success, or are we striving to live a life that aligns with our passions and purpose?

When we take the time to understand what success means to us individually, we can create a roadmap that leads us to our unique destination.

Success Is Commanding Good Results

At its core, success is about commanding good results in succession. It involves consistently striving for improvement and excellence in our endeavors.
Producing positive outcomes is a hallmark of success, whether in our personal lives, careers, or relationships.

As Proverbs 22:29 reminds us, *"Do you see someone skilled in their work? They will serve before kings and not before officials of low rank."* (Proverbs 22:29, NIV)

Think of the farmers who diligently tend to their crops. They understand that success in agriculture is not merely about planting seeds but nurturing them through various stages of growth.

They face challenges such as droughts, pests, and unpredictable weather, yet their commitment to their craft drives them to find solutions and adapt.

Similarly, we must embrace our challenges, viewing them as opportunities to grow and achieve our desired outcomes.

The Role Of Problem-Solving In Success

Success is intricately linked to our ability to solve problems. Every successful individual, regardless of their field, has faced challenges that could have derailed their journey.
However, what distinguishes them is their ability to encounter problems, their resilience, and their determination to find innovative solutions.

They do not shy away from difficulties but view them as opportunities for growth, learning, and transformation.

As the Bible encourages us, *"We also glory in our sufferings, because we know that suffering produces perseverance; perseverance, character; and character, hope."* (Romans 5:3-4, NIV)

The Mindset Of A Problem Solver

At the heart of effective problem-solving is a mindset that embraces challenges. This mindset is characterized by curiosity, creativity, and a willingness to learn.

Successful individuals approach problems with an open mind, recognizing that each challenge presents a unique opportunity to discover something new.

They understand that failures and setbacks are not signs of defeat but integral parts of the learning process.

Identifying and Defining Problems
The first step in effective problem-solving is identifying and clearly defining the problem. Often, individuals encounter situations that seem overwhelming or complex.

However, breaking down these challenges into manageable components can provide clarity and direction.

For instance, consider an entrepreneur facing declining sales. Instead of succumbing to despair, they can analyze the situation to pinpoint the factors contributing to the downturn.

Is it a lack of market awareness?

Are competitors offering better products or prices?

Are customer preferences shifting?

By dissecting the problem into smaller parts, the entrepreneur can develop targeted strategies to address each issue systematically.

Similarly, accurately defining the problem is crucial. Misdiagnosing the issue can lead to ineffective solutions.

For example, a company may perceive its declining sales as a marketing problem when, in reality, it may stem from a lack of product innovation. By taking the time to understand the root causes of a problem, we position ourselves to devise effective solutions.

Embracing Creativity and Innovation
Successful problem solvers often exhibit remarkable creativity and innovation. They understand that traditional solutions may not always suffice, particularly in rapidly changing environments.

As such, they are willing to explore unconventional approaches and think outside the box. Innovation is often born out of necessity. Consider the story of Alexander Graham Bell, who invented the telephone.

His motivation stemmed from a need to communicate with his deaf mother and improve communication with others.

By identifying the problem of limited communication options, Bell dedicated himself to developing a revolutionary solution that changed the world.

The Power of Resilience

Resilience is essential for successful problem-solving. The path to success is rarely linear and often filled with setbacks, failures, and unforeseen challenges.

Resilient individuals possess the tenacity to persevere in the face of adversity. They view obstacles not as insurmountable barriers but as opportunities to learn and grow.

As Scripture reminds us, *"And let us not grow weary of doing good, for in due season we will reap, if we do not give up."* (Galatians 6:9, NIV)

Overcoming Setbacks with Resilience

When faced with a setback, resilient problem solvers do not succumb to negativity or self-doubt.

Instead, they take a step back, evaluate the situation, and adjust their strategies accordingly.
This adaptability allows them to pivot when necessary, ensuring they remain on track toward their goals.

The Bible encourages, *"We also glory in our sufferings, because we know that suffering produces perseverance; perseverance, character; and character, hope."* (Romans 5:3-4, NIV)

Turning Obstacles into Opportunities

For example, consider a startup that encounters unexpected regulatory hurdles.

Rather than abandoning their vision, resilient entrepreneurs analyze the situation, seek expert advice, and adapt their business model to comply.
Through persistence and resourcefulness, they overcome the challenge and may even discover new growth opportunities.

Passion and Purpose in Problem-Solving

Success lies in our ability to solve problems and our love for addressing the issues that matter to us.

Our problem-solving endeavors become more meaningful and impactful when we align our efforts with our values and purpose. As we reflect on our passions, we should ask ourselves: What problems do we genuinely care about solving?

Is it providing a service that enhances people's lives?

Is it advocating for social justice or environmental sustainability?

Is it creating art that inspires others?

The Power of Alignment

For instance, consider social entrepreneurs driven by a desire to address societal challenges.

They identify pressing issues such as poverty, education, or healthcare access and dedicate themselves to finding solutions.

By leveraging their skills and resources, they create innovative programs that make a tangible difference in the lives of others.

Their success is measured not solely by profit but by their positive impact on society.

This alignment of passion and purpose fuels motivation and resilience.

When deeply connected to the problems we are solving, we are more likely to remain committed, even facing challenges.

Our passion drives us to push through obstacles and find creative solutions that contribute to our vision of success.

The Ripple Effect Of Problem-Solving

Solving problems extends beyond our journeys; it creates a ripple effect that can positively impact others.

When we tackle challenges and develop solutions, we benefit ourselves and contribute to the well-being of those around us.

As Proverbs 11:25 reminds us, *"The generous will prosper; those who refresh others will themselves be refreshed."* (Proverbs 11:25, NIV)

For example, when a community leader addresses issues such as food insecurity, they are not only solving a problem for a few individuals. Still, they are potentially transforming the lives of countless families.
Their efforts can inspire others to take action, fostering a culture of collaboration and community support.

We must recognize our potential to create positive change in our personal and professional lives.

By identifying problems within our communities, workplaces, or families and dedicating ourselves to finding solutions, we become catalysts for transformation.

This interconnectedness highlights the importance of empathy and compassion in problem-solving, reminding us that our actions can have far-reaching consequences.

Personal Growth And Development

Another critical aspect of success is personal growth and development. As we journey through life, we must recognize that growth is not merely a destination but an ongoing process. Success requires a commitment to continuous improvement, emotionally, mentally, and spiritually.

To grow personally, we must adopt a mindset of learning. This means being open to new experiences, seeking knowledge, and embracing change. We should view failures not as setbacks but as valuable lessons that contribute to our development. Each experience, whether positive or negative, shapes us into the individuals we are destined to become.

Personal growth often involves stepping outside our comfort zones. It requires us to challenge ourselves, take risks, and confront our fears. When we push beyond our perceived limitations, we discover our true potential and gain the confidence to pursue our goals.

The Connection to Purpose: A more profound sense of purpose lies at the foundation of every significant accomplishment. Purpose is what gives meaning to our actions, guiding us toward the fulfillment of our unique calling. It is not just about setting and achieving goals; it is about understanding "why" we pursue those goals in the first place. When we align our efforts with our God-given purpose, we tap into a reservoir of motivation, passion, and resilience that keeps us moving forward, even when the road becomes difficult. Purpose is the compass that directs our journey, ensuring that every step brings us closer to the life we were meant to live.

The Power of Purpose in Success: Purpose is the driving force behind lasting success. While many people may achieve momentary triumphs based on talent, luck, or external factors, those who operate with a clear purpose create a lasting impact. Purpose fuels our actions with intention. When we clearly understand our purpose, we are not merely working for short-term gains or superficial rewards; we are striving for something more significant that reflects our true essence.

When you look at the lives of highly successful people, one common theme emerges: they are deeply connected to their purpose. Whether they are artists, entrepreneurs, or social advocates, their work is not just a means to an end. It expresses their values, passions, and what they believe they were put on earth to do. They do not simply chase success for its own sake; they pursue goals that align with their purpose, allowing their work to have a profound and lasting impact.

Discovering Your God-Given Purpose: Before fully aligning our efforts with our purpose, we must determine that purpose. This discovery process often involves self-reflection, spiritual introspection, and a willingness to listen to God's guidance.

Our purpose is not something we fabricate; it is revealed to us as we seek to understand our role in the world.

For some, the sense of purpose may come early in life; for others, it may take years of exploration and soul-searching. But no matter the timing, discovering your purpose requires a commitment to seeking clarity and embracing what you feel called to do. This may involve prayer, meditation, or simply reflecting on the passions, talents, and experiences that have shaped your journey so far.

Romans 8:28 reminds us that "*all things work together for good to those who love God, to those who are called according to His purpose.*" This verse reminds us that everything we experience, high and low, shapes our purpose. The challenges we face, the lessons we learn, and the opportunities we embrace all come together to form a tapestry that reflects God's plan for our lives.

Purpose as a Guiding Light: Once we have clarity about our purpose, it becomes a guiding light for everything we do. Purpose provides us with direction and focus, ensuring that we are not aimlessly wandering through life but intentionally pursuing what truly matters. Without a clear sense of purpose, we may find ourselves easily swayed by external pressures, chasing goals that do not align with our values or who we are at our core.

When we are connected to our purpose, our decisions become more intentional. We are not just setting goals to achieve something; we are setting goals aligned with a higher mission. Purpose allows us to discern which opportunities to pursue and which to let go of. It helps us prioritize our time, energy, and resources toward things that bring us closer to the vision we hold for our lives.

For example, consider someone whose purpose is to inspire others through writing. This individual may be presented with many opportunities, some lucrative but unrelated to their calling.

Because they are clear on their purpose, they can easily discern which opportunities align with their mission and which might be distractions. They can say no to things that do not serve their higher purpose, even if they seem appealing on the surface.

Purpose and Perseverance: One of the most significant benefits of being connected to your purpose is the resilience it fosters. Our sense of purpose motivates us to keep going when we encounter obstacles or setbacks. Purpose gives us the strength to persevere, even in adversity, because our efforts are part of something bigger than ourselves.

Challenges can feel overwhelming without a clear sense of purpose, and it becomes easy to give up when things get tough. However, when we are grounded in our purpose, we understand that every challenge is another step toward fulfilling our mission. We are more likely to view setbacks as opportunities for growth, knowing that each obstacle we overcome brings us closer to realizing our goals.

Again, purpose gives us a sense of fulfillment that external success alone cannot offer. Many people chase after achievements, accolades, and recognition, only to feel empty once they attain them. This is because they were not truly aligned with their purpose. On the other hand, when we pursue goals aligned with our purpose, the journey becomes rewarding. Every step we take, no matter how small, contributes to our fulfillment because we know we are aligned with God's plan.

Purpose in Action—Living with Intention: Living with purpose means approaching every aspect of our lives with intention. It means being deliberate about how we spend our time, who we surround ourselves with, and what we invest our energy into. We are not content to live on autopilot when connected to our purpose. Instead, we actively engage with the world around us, making decisions that reflect our values and move us closer to our goals.

This intentionality extends beyond our professional lives; it touches every area of our existence. Our sense of purpose influences our relationships, personal growth, and spiritual development. For instance, someone whose purpose is to serve others may approach their relationships with a mindset of giving rather than taking. They seek to build connections that uplift and empower those around them, knowing that their purpose is tied to the well-being of others.

Similarly, individuals aligned with their purpose are more likely to prioritize personal and spiritual growth. They understand that fulfilling their purpose requires continuous development and are committed to becoming the best versions of themselves to serve their mission more effectively.

Purpose-Driven Success: What am I saying? Success is about achieving external milestones and living a life aligned with your God-given purpose.

Purpose-driven success is lasting because it is rooted in something more profound than material gains or superficial recognition. It is about using your gifts, talents, and resources to contribute to the world in a meaningful way.

When we align with our purpose, success follows naturally. Our work becomes an extension of who we are, and we experience a sense of flow and fulfillment that transcends our challenges. This is the essence of purpose-driven success: a life that is not only prosperous but also meaningful and impactful.

As we progress in this journey, we must continually seek alignment with our purpose. Life will inevitably present distractions and detours, but we can navigate these challenges with clarity and confidence when we remain grounded in our purpose. Success is not just about reaching the destination; it is about walking the path with purpose, knowing that each step brings us closer to the life we were created to live.

Setting Meaningful Goals

We must set meaningful goals that resonate with our values and purpose to achieve success. Goals give us direction and focus and enable us to measure our progress. However, it is essential to ensure our goals are realistic and attainable.

When setting goals, consider using the SMART criteria: *Specific, Measurable, Achievable, Relevant, and Time-bound.* This framework helps us create clear and actionable goals. For instance, instead of saying, "I want to be successful," we might set a goal like, "I will increase my sales by 20% within the next six months." This goal is specific, measurable, achievable, relevant, and time-bound.

Celebrating Milestones: As we work towards our goals, it is crucial to celebrate milestones along the way. Each achievement, no matter how small, is a testament to our progress and dedication. Celebrating milestones fosters a sense of accomplishment and motivates us to keep moving forward.

It is easy to forget our accomplishments in our busy life. However, sustaining an upbeat mindset requires taking the time to recognize our achievements. Celebrating milestones strengthens our dedication to our path, whether by giving ourselves a special treat or sharing our accomplishments with loved ones.

The Power of Resilience: Success is rarely a straight path; it often involves detours, setbacks, and challenges. Bouncing back from adversity is a crucial trait of successful individuals. Resilience enables us to navigate obstacles and remain focused on our goals.

Successful people do not allow themselves to be defeated when faced with difficulties. Instead, they adapt their strategies, learn from their experiences, and continue moving forward. This resilience stems from a strong belief in themselves and their purpose.

As we conclude this chapter, remember that success is not a destination defined by others but a personal journey rooted in your values, goals, and purpose. It is about commanding good results, solving problems, and committing to personal growth. Success is a continuous process of learning, adapting, and thriving.

CHAPTER TWO

UNDERSTANDING YOUR PURPOSE

At the foundation of every successful life is a clear understanding of purpose. Purpose gives our actions meaning and direction. Setting goals and working hard is not enough; true success is achieved when our efforts align with a higher calling, our God-given purpose.

The Importance Of Purpose

The purpose is essential to the human experience. It defines who we are, why we are here, and what we are meant to contribute to the world. Without a sense of purpose, we are like ships without a compass, drifting aimlessly through life. We may achieve temporary success, but it will feel hollow without a deeper understanding of why we do what we do.

Connecting with your purpose brings clarity. It helps you understand what you should be doing and how to direct your talents, time, and resources toward the things that matter most. Purpose is what motivates us to keep going when things get tough. It is a steadying force that gives us direction and confidence, ensuring we remain focused on what is truly important.

Proverbs 19:21 reminds us, "*There are many plans in a man's heart, nevertheless the Lord's counsel—that will stand.*" We may have our ambitions and desires, but God's purpose for our lives ultimately prevails. When we align our plans with His purpose, we work toward success and fulfill our divine calling.

Discovering Your Divine Purpose

Discovering your purpose is often a journey of self-reflection, spiritual growth, and surrender to God's guidance. It requires looking beyond societal expectations and superficial definitions of success to understand the unique role that God has designed for you. Everyone has a divine purpose, but uncovering it requires intentional seeking.

One of the key ways to discover your purpose is through prayer and meditation. By seeking God's will for your life, you open yourself up to His direction and wisdom. It is essential to approach this process with humility, asking God to reveal His plan for you rather than trying to force your desires into His will. Jeremiah 29:11 assures us of God's good intentions: "*For I know the plans I have for you, says the Lord, plans to prosper you and not to harm you, plans to give you a future and a hope.*"

Your purpose may also be revealed through the unique gifts, talents, and passions that God has placed within you. Often, the things you are naturally drawn to, whether serving others, creating art, solving complex problems, or leading people, offer clues about your purpose. Pay attention to what energizes you and brings you joy. These are often indicators of where God calls you to make a difference.

In addition, reflecting on your life experiences can provide insight into your purpose. Our greatest struggles, challenges, and breakthroughs are often connected to the mission God has for us. What have you learned from your past? What obstacles have you overcome? The answers to these questions can point you toward your purpose, showing how God has equipped you to use your experiences to bless others.

The Role Of Faith In Connecting With Your Purpose

Faith is an essential component in understanding and living out your purpose. We may often have an idea of our purpose, but it may seem too big or overwhelming to pursue. This is where faith steps in. Faith allows us to trust that God's plan is more significant than our fears or limitations. It gives us the courage to step into our calling, even when uncertain.

In Hebrews 11:1, we are reminded that *"faith is the substance of things hoped for, the evidence of things not seen."* Living with purpose often requires faith because we cannot always see the complete picture of where God is leading us. Yet, when we trust in His guidance, we can take bold steps toward fulfilling our mission.

It's essential to recognize that living out your purpose may not always be easy. There will be moments of doubt, confusion, and difficulty. However, it is during these times that our faith is tested and strengthened. As we walk in faith, God reveals more of His plan for our lives, giving us the wisdom and strength to overcome obstacles and stay true to our purpose.

Faith also reminds us that our purpose is not just about achieving personal success but glorifying God and serving others. When we approach our work and goals with a heart of service, we fulfill the greatest commandment: to love God and others - Matthew 22:37-39. This perspective shifts our focus from simply pursuing individual success to positively impacting the world around us.

Aligning Your Goals With Your Purpose

Once you understand your purpose, the next step is to align your goals with that purpose. Too often, people set goals based on external expectations, which society deems successful, without considering whether those goals align with their divine calling. While achieving worldly success may bring temporary satisfaction, true fulfillment comes when our goals reflect our purpose.

Examine your current pursuits to ensure your goals align with your purpose. Ask yourself: Are these goals moving me closer to the life God has called me to live? Are they aligned with my core values and passions? Am I pursuing them out of genuine desire or a need for approval or validation from others?

One effective way to align your goals with your purpose is using the SMART criteria: *Specific, Measurable, Achievable, Relevant, and Time-bound.* While this is a practical goal-setting framework, focusing on the "relevant" aspect is the key to making it purposeful. Relevance means that the goal is practical and aligned with your divine purpose. When your goals are relevant to your purpose, you will find that they bring more profound satisfaction and motivation as they resonate with who you are and what you were created to do.

For example, if your purpose is to help others, setting a goal to mentor five individuals in the next six months is a clear, purposeful objective. If your purpose is to create, setting a goal to write and publish a book that reflects your values and experiences would be a meaningful pursuit. When our goals are directly tied to our purpose, we are more likely to stay committed and resilient in facing challenges.

Living With Intention

Purpose-driven living requires a high degree of intentionality. When we are clear about our purpose, we are less likely to waste time on pursuits that do not serve us—every decision we make and action we take reflects our commitment to living out our purpose.

Living with intention also means being present at the moment and making the most of the opportunities God places before us. It's easy to get caught up in the hustle and bustle of life, constantly looking toward the next goal or achievement. But living purposefully requires us to slow down and fully engage with the present. When we are present, we are more attuned to God's guidance and better able to discern His will for our lives.

Intentionality also extends to the relationships we nurture. The people we surround ourselves with can support or hinder our journey toward fulfilling our purpose. Building relationships that encourage growth, provide accountability, and align with our values is essential. Proverbs 27:17 reminds us, "*As iron sharpens iron, so one person sharpens another.*" Surround yourself with people who challenge you to grow spiritually, mentally, and emotionally, as they will play a key role in helping you stay focused on your purpose.

Overcoming Distractions And Detours

One of the biggest challenges in living out our purpose is avoiding distractions and detours. The enemy often uses distractions to pull us away from our God-given mission.

These distractions can take many forms, such as materialism, comparison, fear, and even well-meaning but misaligned opportunities. It's easy to get sidetracked when the world offers many paths to success, but not all lead to fulfillment.

To overcome distractions, we must stay grounded in our purpose. This requires regular self-reflection and prayer, asking God to reveal whether we are still on the right path or need to realign. It's also helpful to have a support system, whether it's a mentor, pastor, or trusted friend, who can provide guidance and help you stay focused on your mission.

When distractions arise, remember that God's timing is perfect. Sometimes, we may feel tempted to rush ahead or pursue shortcuts to success, but true purpose-driven success requires patience and perseverance. Trust that God works behind the scenes, orchestrating everything for your good and His glory. Psalm 37:23 reminds us, "*The Lord orders the steps of a good man, and He delights in his way.*"

Living a life of purpose is a journey of faith, intention, and alignment. Understanding our divine purpose empowers us to set meaningful goals, overcome distractions, and live with a sense of fulfillment beyond temporary achievements. Purpose is not something we create; it is something we discover as we seek God's will.

As you progress in your journey, remember that your purpose is unique. Do not compare your path to others or measure your success by worldly standards. Instead, trust that God has a specific plan for your life that will bring you peace, joy, and success as you walk in alignment with His will. Your purpose is your greatest asset, and when you live by it, you are not only becoming successful, you are becoming the person God created you to be.

The Importance Of Destiny In Achieving Success

Destiny is a powerful concept that shapes our lives and guides us toward our ultimate purpose. It goes beyond personal ambition and superficial goals; it speaks to God's more profound spiritual plan for us. Our destiny is not just about what we want to achieve but about aligning ourselves with the path God has designed for us.

Destiny Versus Ambition

One of the most critical distinctions is the difference between destiny and ambition. While ambition is often driven by personal desires, external validation, or societal expectations, destiny is rooted in a higher calling. Ambition focuses on what we want for ourselves, while destiny focuses on what God wants. Ambition can sometimes lead us down paths that may seem successful in the short term but ultimately leave us unfulfilled. In contrast, following our destiny leads to lasting success, peace, and a sense of accomplishment that transcends worldly definitions of achievement.

A desire for fame, wealth, or power can often drive ambition. It is based on our limited perspective of what success looks like. However, when we chase ambition without understanding our destiny, we risk pursuing goals that do not align with who we are meant to be. This can lead to frustration, burnout, and a lack of fulfillment.

On the other hand, when we pursue our destiny, we are walking in alignment with God's plan for our lives. Our actions become purposeful, our goals become meaningful, and our success reflects the destiny we are fulfilling.

As Proverbs 16:9 reminds us, "*A man's heart plans his way, but the Lord directs his steps.*" While ambition can drive us to make plans, God's direction ultimately leads us to success. Understanding and accepting this truth allows us to surrender our ambitions and trust that God's plan for our destiny will lead us to true success.

Destiny as a Destination

Destiny is often considered a destination where we are meant to arrive. However, it is essential to recognize that destiny is both a journey and a destination. Every step we take and every decision we make is part of walking toward our destiny. Success is about reaching the final destination and embracing the journey that leads us there.

God has a specific plan for each of us, and that plan is intricately woven into the fabric of our lives. Our destiny begins to unfold from the moment we are born.

Our experiences, the people we meet, and the challenges we face all shape our destiny. Sometimes, we may feel we are far from our destination, but every step we take brings us closer to fulfilling our destiny.

It is important to remember that destiny is not something we create; it is something we discover. As we walk through life, we must remain open to the guidance of the Holy Spirit, who reveals our destiny to us in His timing. This requires patience, faith, and a willingness to trust that God is leading us exactly where we need to go. Psalm 37:23 assures us, *"The Lord orders the steps of a good man, and He delights in his way."* When we trust that God directs our steps, we can confidently move forward, knowing that our destiny is secure.

Living with a Sense of Destiny
Living with a sense of destiny means understanding that your life has a greater purpose and that you are meant to achieve something extraordinary.

When you have a clear sense of destiny, you begin to interpret your experiences, choices, and relationships through the lens of that purpose. This perspective gives you the confidence and determination to keep moving forward, even when obstacles arise.

One key benefit of living with a sense of destiny is its clarity. When you know where you are headed, you are less likely to be distracted by irrelevant pursuits or tempted to follow paths that lead away from your true calling.

Every decision you make is filtered through the understanding of where you are destined to go, allowing you to stay focused and aligned with God's plan for your life.

Living with a sense of destiny also brings a sense of urgency and intention to everything you do. You recognize that your time on earth is limited and that each day is an opportunity to move closer to fulfilling your destiny. This sense of purpose motivates you to make the most of every moment, ensuring your actions are intentional and meaningful.

In addition, living with a sense of destiny helps you build solid values and make better decisions. You are less likely to make impulsive or short-sighted choices when guided by your destiny. Instead, you focus on what will bring you closer to your long-term goals and what aligns with the values God has placed in your heart. This clarity strengthens your decision-making process and allows you to take the right actions at the right time.

Destiny and the Role of Faith

Faith is central to understanding and fulfilling our destiny. Without faith, it is easy to become discouraged or overwhelmed by our challenges. However, when we believe in God's plan, we can trust He is working everything for our good, even when we don't fully understand the process.

Fulfilling your destiny often requires taking steps of faith, even when the path is unclear. In Hebrews 11:8, we see an example of this in Abraham's life: *"By faith, Abraham obeyed when he was called to go out to the place which he would receive as an inheritance. And he went out, not knowing where he was going."*

Like Abraham, we may not always know where God is leading us, but faith gives us the courage to take the next step, trusting that God will reveal the rest of the journey in His timing.

Faith also reminds us that we do not achieve our destiny alone. It is a partnership between us and God. While we are called to work diligently and make wise decisions, God ultimately brings our destiny to fruition. This understanding frees us from the pressure of trying to control every aspect of our lives and allows us to rest in the knowledge that God is in control.

Overcoming Obstacles on the Path to Destiny

Every journey toward fulfilling our destiny will include obstacles. These obstacles are not meant to deter us but to strengthen and prepare us for the greater purpose ahead. When we encounter challenges, we must view them as opportunities for growth and development, trusting that God is using them to shape us into the people we need to be to fulfill our destiny.

One of the most common obstacles people face on the path to destiny is fear. Fear of failure, fear of the unknown, and fear of inadequacy can all prevent us from stepping into our calling.

However, 2 Timothy 1:7 reminds us, *"For God has not given us a spirit of fear, but of power and love and a sound mind."* When we live with a sense of destiny, we recognize that fear has no place in our journey. Instead, we are empowered by the Holy Spirit to move forward with boldness and confidence.

Another obstacle that can hinder us from fulfilling our destiny is doubt. Doubt often arises when we face setbacks or when the journey feels longer than expected. In these moments, we must remind ourselves of God's faithfulness.

Psalm 138:8 encourages us, *"The Lord will fulfill his purpose for me; your steadfast love, O Lord, endures forever."* Even when we cannot see the whole picture, we can trust that God is still working behind the scenes to bring our destiny to pass.

Distractions are another challenge that can pull us away from our path. In a world filled with noise and competing priorities, losing sight of our true calling is easy. This is why it is so important to stay connected to God through prayer, meditation, and studying His word. By maintaining a close relationship with God, we can discern which opportunities align with our destiny and which are simply distractions.

The Role Of Relationships In Fulfilling Destiny

The people we surround ourselves with are also important in our journey toward fulfilling our destiny. God often uses relationships to guide us, support us, and open doors of opportunity. Proverbs 27:17 says, *"As iron sharpens iron, so one man sharpens another."*

The right relationships can help sharpen our character, provide wisdom, and hold us accountable as we pursue our goals.

However, not all relationships are beneficial for our journey. Toxic or damaging relationships can introduce and pull us away from our destiny. We must surround ourselves with people who share our values, encourage growth, and support our vision. These are the relationships that God uses to propel us forward.

At the same time, we must be mindful of the people we allow to speak into our lives. Not everyone will understand your destiny or the path God has called you to walk. This is why it is essential to seek guidance from spiritually mature people aligned with God's purpose for your life.

Having a mentor or spiritual advisor can provide valuable insight and encouragement as you navigate the challenges and opportunities on your journey toward fulfilling your destiny.

Understanding your destiny is critical to achieving true success. It goes beyond personal ambition and aligns your life with God's plan. Living with a sense of destiny empowers you to make intentional choices, overcome obstacles, and stay focused on your long-term goals. Destiny gives your life meaning, purpose, and direction, ensuring personal and impactful success.

As you progress in your journey, remember that your destiny is unique. Trust that God has a specific plan for your life, and be willing to take steps of faith as He reveals that plan to you.

You do not achieve your destiny through your strength alone; it is a partnership with God. By embracing your destiny and living in alignment with His will, you will reach success far beyond worldly accomplishments.

CHAPTER THREE

THE JOURNEY TO SUCCESS: SETTING AND ACHIEVING YOUR GOALS

S uccess is not a singular event but a continuous journey shaped by the goals we set and our commitment to achieving them. Setting goals is the first step toward transforming our vision of success into reality. However, it is not enough to simply set goals; we must also develop a plan to achieve them and be disciplined to stay the course, even when challenges arise.

The Importance Of Setting Goals

Setting goals is the foundation of any success story. Without clear goals, we are like travelers with no destination, wandering through life without a sense of direction. Goals structure our journey, allowing us to focus our efforts and measure our progress. As Proverbs 29:18 reminds us, "*Where there is no vision, the people perish.*"

Having a vision for your life and setting goals to fulfill that vision is essential for achieving success.

Goals give us clarity. They help us break down our larger aspirations into manageable steps, making the path to success more attainable. We can better prioritize our time, energy, and resources when we have clear, well-defined goals. Instead of being overwhelmed by the enormity of our dreams, we can focus on the smaller, actionable steps that bring us closer to our desired outcome.

Setting goals also creates a sense of purpose and motivation. When we know what we are working toward, we are more likely to stay committed, even when the journey becomes difficult. Goals give us something to strive for, reminding us that every effort contributes to a larger mission.

Setting Smart Goals

Not all goals are created equal.
Setting specific, measurable, achievable, relevant, and time-bound goals (SMART) is crucial for increasing our chances of success.
The SMART framework is a powerful tool for ensuring our goals are clear, realistic, and aligned with our purpose.

As Proverbs 4:26 reminds us, *"Give careful thought to the paths for your feet and be steadfast in all your ways."* (Proverbs 4:26, NIV)

Specific: Defining Your Target
Your goals should be precise and clearly defined.
Instead of vague aspirations like "I want to be successful," make your goals specific.

For example, "I want to increase my sales by 20% within the next six months" provides a clear target to work toward.

Measurable: Tracking Progress
Having a way to track progress is essential.
Measurable goals allow you to see how far you've come and

whether you're on track to achieve your desired outcome.

For example, when increasing sales, regularly reviewing sales data enables you to measure progress.

Achievable: Balancing Ambition and Reality
While dreaming big is vital, your goals should also be realistic.

Setting achievable goals prevents discouragement and ensures incremental progress.

Break down larger goals into smaller, manageable steps.

Relevant: Aligning with Purpose
Your goals should align with your broader purpose and values.

Before setting a goal, ask yourself: Is this goal relevant to my long-term vision?

Will achieving this goal bring me closer to fulfilling my purpose?

Does it align with the path God has called me to walk?

As Psalm 37:23 reminds us, *"The Lord makes firm the steps of the one who delights in him."* (Psalm 37:23, NIV)

Time-bound: Creating Urgency
Every goal needs a deadline or timeframe.
Without a sense of urgency, procrastination and distraction can occur.

Setting a specific timeline for achieving your goal keeps you accountable and committed to consistent action.

By setting SMART goals, you create a roadmap that guides you toward success. Each goal becomes a milestone, bringing you closer to your ultimate vision.

Aligning Your Goals With Your Purpose

One of the most critical aspects of goal setting is ensuring that your goals are aligned with your divine purpose. It is easy to become distracted by external pressures or societal expectations, but true success comes when our goals reflect the path God has set for us.

Before setting any goal, reflect on your purpose and values. What has God placed in your heart? What are the unique talents, passions, and gifts that He has given you? Your goals should reflect these more profound truths. When your goals align with your purpose, you will find that achieving them brings a sense of fulfillment and peace beyond mere external success.

For example, if your purpose is to serve others, your goals should reflect that mission. Setting a goal to mentor a certain number of individuals or to launch a community service initiative would be aligned with your purpose.

On the other hand, setting a goal purely for financial gain, without considering its impact on others or how it aligns with your values, may lead to success in the eyes of the world but leave you feeling unfulfilled.

Psalm 37:4 says, "*Delight yourself also in the Lord, and He shall give you the desires of your heart.*" When you delight in God and align your goals with His will, you pursue personal success and fulfill His greater purpose for your life.

Breaking Down Goals Into Actionable Steps

Once you have set clear, purposeful goals, the next step is to break them down into smaller, actionable tasks. Significant goals can sometimes feel overwhelming, but dividing them into manageable steps creates a clear path forward.

For example, if your goal is to write a book, the task may initially seem daunting. However, you make the goal more attainable by breaking it down into smaller steps, such as writing one chapter per week or setting a daily word count. Each step brings you closer to the outcome, and with each completed task, you build momentum.

This process of breaking down goals also allows you to stay focused on what needs to be done in the present moment. Instead of worrying about the final result, you can concentrate on completing the task, trusting that each small step contributes to the larger goal.

Staying Committed And Overcoming Challenges

The journey to success is rarely smooth. You will encounter obstacles, setbacks, and moments of doubt. However, staying committed to your goals despite challenges separates those who achieve success from those who give up.

One of the most important qualities for achieving your goals is resilience. Resilience allows you to bounce back from failure, learn from your mistakes, and keep moving forward. James 1:12 encourages us, *"Blessed is the man who remains steadfast under trial, for when he has stood the test, he will receive the crown of life."* Trials are inevitable, but it is through perseverance that we ultimately achieve success.

When challenges arise, it is essential to remember why you set your goals in the first place. Returning to your purpose and vision can reignite your motivation and remind you of the greater mission you are working toward. Prayer and meditation can also provide clarity and strength during difficult times, helping you stay focused on God's plan for your life.

It is also essential to be flexible in your approach. While your goals should remain consistent, the path to achieving them may need to be adjusted along the way.

Life is unpredictable, and sometimes, our plans do not unfold as we expect. Adapting and finding new ways to move forward is crucial in these moments. You can navigate obstacles and progress toward your goals by remaining open to change and trusting God's guidance.

As you work toward achieving your goals, it is essential to celebrate the milestones you reach along the way. Every small victory is a testament to your progress and dedication. Celebrating these moments reinforces your commitment and motivates you to strive for success.

Sometimes, we become so focused on the outcome that we forget to acknowledge our progress. However, reflecting on and celebrating your achievements is an essential part of the journey. Whether completing a project, reaching a financial milestone, or achieving personal growth, each step forward is worth recognizing.

Similarly, celebrating milestones allows you to express gratitude for the blessings and opportunities that God has provided. Gratitude is a powerful force that shifts our focus from what we have yet to accomplish to what we have already achieved. By practicing gratitude, we cultivate a positive mindset that encourages further success.

The Role Of Accountability

Achieving your goals is not something you have to do alone. An accountability partner or mentor can provide invaluable support and guidance on your journey. An accountability partner can help keep you on track, offer encouragement when you face challenges, and provide constructive feedback as you work toward your goals.

Proverbs 27:17 says, "*As iron sharpens iron, so one person sharpens another.*" Surrounding yourself with people who share your values and support your vision can strengthen your resolve and help you stay focused. Whether it's a trusted friend, family member, or spiritual mentor, having someone to hold you accountable increases your chances of success.

Accountability can also come in the form of self-discipline. Setting up systems to track your progress and hold yourself accountable can help you stay on course. Whether using a journal, creating a checklist, or setting reminders, these tools can help you stay organized and committed to achieving your goals.

Setting and achieving goals is a vital part of the journey to success. It provides direction, motivation, and a clear path forward. However, it is not enough to set goals; we must also ensure that our goals are aligned with our purpose and are broken down into actionable steps. Staying committed, celebrating milestones, and seeking accountability are essential to realizing our goals.

Overcoming Obstacles And Failures

Success is often seen as a straight path, where each step leads to more remarkable achievement. However, the journey to success is full of obstacles and failures. These challenges are not meant to deter us but to strengthen us, helping us build the resilience and wisdom necessary for lasting success.

The Reality of Obstacles

No one reaches success without facing obstacles. These obstacles can take different forms, such as personal struggles, financial hardships, professional setbacks, or unexpected life events. Yet, these challenges are not a reflection of failure but part of the journey. Overcoming obstacles often distinguishes truly successful individuals from those who give up.

It is essential to acknowledge that obstacles are inevitable. The key is how we respond to them. In James 1:2-4, we are reminded to *"count it all joy when you fall into various trials, knowing that testing your faith produces patience. But let patience have its perfect work, that you may be perfect and complete, lacking nothing."* Obstacles are not meant to break us; they are growth opportunities. They test our faith, build patience, and equip us with the strength we need for the next stage of our journey.

Obstacles also teach us valuable lessons. When we face difficulties, we must examine our strategies, rethink our approach, and, often, adjust our mindset. Without obstacles, we might continue down paths that are not serving us, pursuing goals not aligned with our true purpose. Challenges act as checkpoints, prompting us to reflect, reassess, and realign ourselves with God's life plan.

The Role of Failure in Success

Failure is often viewed as the opposite of success, but failure is a critical component of the success journey. Every successful individual has faced failure at some point, and often, multiple times. The difference is that successful people do not let failure define them; they use it as a stepping stone to tremendous success.

In the Bible, we see many examples of individuals who faced failure but ultimately fulfilled their purpose. One such example is Peter's story. After denying Jesus three times, Peter could have given up on his calling. But instead, he repented, learned from his failure, and became one of the key figures in the early Christian church. His story is a powerful reminder that failure is not final. As Proverbs 24:16 says, *"For though the righteous fall seven times, they rise again."*

Failure teaches us humility. It reminds us that we are imperfect and will make mistakes. However, we are most open to learning and growth in these moments of humility. Acknowledging our failures gives us valuable insight into what went wrong and how we can improve. Failure is a teacher, not a punishment. It allows us to refine our approach, strengthen our resolve, and ultimately achieve tremendous success.

It's also important to recognize that failure often opens doors to new opportunities. What may seem like a setback at the moment could be the very thing that leads us to a breakthrough. When we trust God's plan, we see that our failures serve a purpose.

Romans 8:28 assures us, *"And we know that in all things God works for the good of those who love him, who have been called according to his purpose."* Every failure and obstacle is part of the more remarkable story that God is writing in our lives.

Embracing A Growth Mindset

To overcome obstacles and failures, we must develop a growth mindset. This mindset, popularized by psychologist Carol Dweck, is the belief that our abilities and intelligence can be developed through effort, learning, and perseverance. A growth mindset sees failure as a natural part of learning, not a reflection of our worth or capabilities.

When we approach challenges with a growth mindset, we are more likely to embrace them as growth opportunities rather than threats to our success. We become more resilient, adaptable, and open to feedback. This mindset allows us to persist despite setbacks and continue striving toward our goals, even when the road is difficult.

A growth mindset is deeply aligned with biblical principles. Scripture shows examples of individuals who faced significant challenges but grew more assertive. In Philippians 3:13-14, Paul writes, *"But one thing I do: Forgetting what is behind and straining toward what is ahead, I press on toward the goal to win the prize for which God has called me heavenward in Christ Jesus."* This scripture reflects the essence of a growth mindset, focusing on what lies ahead, learning from past experiences, and pressing forward toward the goal.

The Need For Substance In Success

Success is more than just reaching goals or acquiring wealth. True success has depth, meaning, and substance. Achieving outward success is not enough if there is no substance behind it. Substance in success refers to the character, values, and principles that support our achievements. Without substance, success is shallow and fleeting.

One of the most essential components of substance is integrity. Success built on lies, manipulation, or unethical behavior is not true success. It may lead to temporary gains, but it will eventually crumble.

Integrity ensures our success is built on a solid foundation that honors God and reflects our values. Proverbs 10:9 says, *"Whoever walks in integrity walks securely, but whoever takes crooked paths will be found out."* Integrity is the cornerstone of lasting success.

Substance in success also means having a sense of purpose. As we discussed earlier, success without purpose is empty. We add meaning to our achievements by aligning our goals with our God-given purpose. Each milestone reflects the greater mission we are fulfilling, giving us a sense of fulfillment that goes beyond material success.

Another critical aspect of substance is humility. Humility keeps us grounded, reminding us that our success is not achieved through our efforts alone but through God's grace. It allows us to remain teachable, open to feedback, and willing to grow. In James 4:10, we are reminded to *"Humble yourselves before the Lord, and he will lift you."* True success is marked by humility, as it acknowledges that we are instruments of God's will and that our accomplishments are ultimately for His glory.

Building A Strong Foundation

To achieve success with substance, we must build a strong foundation. This foundation is rooted in our relationship with God, values, and commitment to personal growth. Without a solid foundation, external circumstances make success fragile and easily shaken.

The parable of the wise and foolish builders in Matthew 7:24-27 demonstrates the importance of building on a solid foundation. The wise builder constructs his house on rock, while the foolish builder builds his house on sand. When the storms come, the house built on rock stands firm, while the built on sand collapses. This parable is a powerful reminder that our success must be built on the rock of God's truth, not the shifting sands of worldly success.

Building a solid foundation also requires discipline. Success does not happen accidentally; it results from consistent effort, discipline, and commitment. Discipline helps us stay focused on our goals, resist distractions, and continue working even when we don't feel motivated. Hebrews 12:11 reminds us, "*No discipline seems pleasant at the time, but painful. Later on, however, it produces a harvest of righteousness and peace for those trained by it.*" Discipline is not always easy, but it is necessary for achieving success with substance.

Overcoming setbacks and hurdles is a vital component of the success journey. These difficulties are intended to hone us, deepen our faith, and set us up for success rather than depress us. By adopting a growth mentality, strengthening our resilience, and upholding our integrity, we may face challenges with poise and assurance.

True success is not just about achieving goals; it is about building a life of substance that reflects our values, honors God, and fulfills our purpose. As you

CHAPTER FOUR

GOD'S EXPECTATION FOR YOUR SUCCESS

Success is often viewed through a personal lens, characterized by individual goals, ambitions, and achievements. However, true success transcends our desires and is deeply intertwined with God's expectations for our lives. Aligning our pursuits with God's plan and timing enhances our chances of success and ensures that our achievements have lasting significance.

Understanding God's Plan For Your Life

From our creation, God has a unique plan for each of us. Jeremiah 29:11 captures this truth beautifully: *"For I know the plans I have for you, declares the Lord, plans to prosper you and not to harm you, plans to give you hope and a future."* This verse emphasizes that God's plans are rooted in love and intention, designed to lead us toward a life of fulfillment and purpose.

However, understanding God's plan for our lives requires a willingness to seek Him earnestly. It is not enough to assume we know what God wants; we must actively pursue a relationship with Him, asking for guidance and clarity. Through prayer, meditation, and studying Scripture, we open ourselves up to divine revelation.

In seeking God's plan, we often discover that our vision for success may not always align with His. While we may have specific goals and desires, God's plans usually exceed our understanding. His perspective encompasses the entirety of our lives, and He sees the bigger picture, which may include challenges and detours that ultimately lead us to our true purpose.

The Importance Of Surrender

Aligning with God's plan requires a spirit of surrender. Surrendering means letting go of our need to control every aspect of our lives and trusting that God knows what is best for us. This can be difficult, especially when our plans do not unfold as we envisioned. However, surrender is an act of faith, acknowledging that God's wisdom surpasses our own.

In Matthew 16:24-25, Jesus teaches, "*If anyone desires to come after Me, let him deny himself, take up his cross, and follow Me. For whoever desires to save his life will lose it, but whoever loses his life for My sake will find it.*" This scripture explains the essence of surrender, putting aside our ambitions to follow God's leading. When we surrender our plans to Him, we create space for Him to work in our lives and guide us toward the success He has in store.

Surrendering does not mean abandoning our goals; instead, it involves holding them loosely and being open to God's redirection. As we walk in faith, we may find that God takes us down unexpected paths, leading us to opportunities and experiences that we could never have imagined. These divine detours are often essential for our growth and success.

Recognizing God's Timing

Timing is another critical element that aligns with God's plan. We live in a fast-paced world that often demands immediate results and quick success. However, God's timing operates on a different schedule, one that is perfect and intentional. Ecclesiastes 3:1 reminds us, *"To everything, there is a season, a time for every purpose under heaven."*

Understanding God's timing requires patience and trust. Sometimes, we feel impatient, wondering why our goals are not being fulfilled as quickly as we desire. In these moments, we must remember that our timelines do not bind God. His timing is rooted in His perfect wisdom and love for us.

God may delay specific outcomes because He prepares us for what lies ahead. Perhaps we need more time to grow in character, develop skills, or build resilience. The challenges we face during waiting periods are not wasted time; they are essential parts of our journey that shape us into the individuals God intends us to be.

Consider the story of Joseph in the Old Testament. After being sold into slavery by his brothers and falsely imprisoned, Joseph endured years of hardship before eventually rising to power in Egypt. God's timing in Joseph's life was perfect, orchestrating events that saved many lives during a severe famine. Joseph's journey was marked by waiting, but through it all, he remained faithful to God's plan. When the time was right, God elevated him to a position of influence.

The Power Of Prayer

Prayer is vital in aligning our lives with God's plan and timing. We communicate with God through prayer, seeking His guidance, wisdom, and clarity regarding our goals. We can express our desires through prayer while remaining open to His leadership.

In Philippians 4:6-7, Paul encourages us: *"Be anxious for nothing, but in everything by prayer and supplication, with thanksgiving, let your requests be made known to God; and the peace of God, which surpasses all understanding, will guard your hearts and minds through Christ Jesus."* This passage signifies the importance of prayer in relieving anxiety and finding peace amid uncertainty.

We invite Him into our plans and aspirations when we pray to God. We can ask for His direction, wisdom, and timing in our pursuits. As we pray, we must also be attentive to His voice, allowing the Holy Spirit to guide our thoughts and decisions. God may speak to us through Scripture, the counsel of trusted mentors, or the gentle promptings of the Holy Spirit.

Trusting In God's Provision

Aligning with God's plan also involves trusting in His provision. When we commit our goals and desires to Him, we can rest assured that He will provide the resources, opportunities, and strength we need to fulfill our purpose. This requires a deep level of faith, knowing that God is willing and able to equip us for the journey ahead.

Matthew 6:33 reminds us, "*But seek first the kingdom of God and His righteousness, and all these things shall be added to you.*" When we prioritize our relationship with God and seek to align our lives with His will, we open the door for His provision. God knows our needs and desires and promises to provide for us as we faithfully pursue His plan.

Trusting in God's provision also means letting go of the desire to control every outcome. We may encounter setbacks, uncertainties, or closed doors along the way, but when we trust in God's plan, we can view these challenges as opportunities for growth and redirection. Just as a gardener prunes a plant to encourage healthy growth, God sometimes removes obstacles to help us flourish in our purpose.

Building Character Through Challenges

God's expectations for our success extend beyond achieving our goals; they encompass our character development. Success is defined by what we accomplish and who we become. As we align our plans with God's will, we must also be willing to undergo the refining process that shapes our character.

James 1:2-4 encourages us, "*My brethren, count it all joy when you fall into various trials, knowing that testing your faith produces patience. But let patience have its perfect work, that you may be perfect and complete, lacking nothing.*"

Challenges are often opportunities for character development. When we face difficulties, we must rely on God's strength, learn perseverance, and cultivate patience, humility, and empathy.

The journey to success is not always linear; it may involve detours and unexpected challenges. However, each trial is an opportunity for growth. We develop resilience and a deeper understanding of ourselves as we handle obstacles. God uses these experiences to prepare us for greater responsibilities and to help us become the individuals He has called us to be.

Embracing God's Expectations

Understanding God's expectations for our success requires humility and a willingness to submit our plans to His authority. It is essential to approach our pursuits with an attitude of servanthood, recognizing that our lives are not solely for our benefit but for the glory of God and the service of others.

In Romans 12:1, Paul urges us, "*I beseech you therefore, brethren, by the mercies of God, that you present your bodies a living sacrifice, holy, acceptable to God, which is your reasonable service.*" This verse emphasizes the importance of surrendering our ambitions and desires to God. When we present ourselves as living sacrifices, we align our lives with His expectations and allow Him to work through us for His purpose.

Embracing God's expectations also means being open to His leading, even when it challenges our comfort zones or disrupts our plans. The journey of success is not about seeking our glory but glorifying God in all we do. When we align our pursuits with His plan, success takes on a deeper meaning, reflecting our commitment to serving others and honoring God.

Aligning with God's plan and timing is essential for achieving true success. It requires a heart willing to surrender, a commitment to prayer, and a readiness to trust God's provision. By seeking to understand God's expectations, we can walk confidently on the path He has laid out for us.

Success is not merely about reaching goals; it is about becoming the person God created you to be and fulfilling the divine calling in your life. Embrace God's expectations, trust His timing, and walk confidently in His plan. Your journey to success is not just about the destination; it is about the transformation that occurs along the way, shaping you into a vessel of His love, grace, and power.

The Importance Of Humility And Integrity

Achievements, wealth, and recognition often define success in life. However, true success is much more resounding than these external markers. It is rooted in character and values, particularly humility and integrity. As we journey toward success, understanding the significance of these qualities in the context of God's expectations is essential for aligning our lives with His plan and fulfilling our divine purpose.

Understanding Humility
Humility is the quality of humility; it involves recognizing our limitations, valuing others, and placing God at the center of our lives. In a world that often celebrates self-promotion and individualism, humility can be a counter-cultural value that sets us apart as followers of Christ. Philippians 2:3 encourages us: "*Let nothing be done through selfish ambition or conceit, but in lowliness of mind let each esteem others better than himself.*"

Humility allows us to remain teachable and open to growth.

When we embrace a humble mindset, we acknowledge that we do not have all the answers. We recognize that we need God's guidance and the wisdom of others to handle the complexities of life. Humility promotes a willingness to listen, learn, and adapt, which is vital for success.

In addition, humility encourages collaboration and healthy relationships. When we are humble, we are more inclined to serve others and prioritize their needs above our own. This servant leadership model aligns with the teachings of Jesus, who demonstrated the ultimate act of humility by washing His disciples' feet - John 13:1-17. By embodying humility, we create an environment that fosters trust, cooperation, and mutual respect.

The Role Of Integrity In Success

Integrity is the quality of being honest and having strong moral principles. It is the foundation upon which true success is built. Maintaining integrity is crucial for achieving lasting success in a world where shortcuts and dishonesty can sometimes lead to temporary gains. Proverbs 11:3 states, *"The integrity of the upright will guide them, but the perversity of the unfaithful will destroy them."* This verse signifies that integrity leads us on the right path, while lacking it ultimately leads to ruin.

Living with integrity means being consistent in our actions, words, and values. It involves aligning our decisions with our beliefs and ensuring we act honestly, even when no one is watching. Integrity builds trust, both with God and with others. When people see us as trustworthy and honest, they are more likely to support and respect us.

Integrity also plays a significant part in our relationship with God. When we live with integrity, we honor Him and reflect His character to the world. God desires us to be people of integrity, and our faithfulness in small matters lays the groundwork for greater responsibilities. Luke 16:10 reminds us, *"He who is faithful in what is least is faithful also in much."*

Humility and Integrity in Action

To truly embody humility and integrity, we must implement these values in our daily lives. This means being mindful of our attitudes, choices, and interactions with others. For example, in the workplace, practicing humility might involve acknowledging the contributions of our team members and valuing their input. It could also mean being willing to admit our mistakes and learn from them rather than trying to cover them up or shift blame.

Similarly, integrity should guide our decision-making processes. When faced with ethical dilemmas or difficult choices, we must pause and ask ourselves: "What would align with my values? What would God want me to do?" This approach ensures that our actions are consistent with our beliefs and reinforces our commitment to integrity.

Similarly, humility and integrity involve transparency in our dealings with others. This transparency builds trust and fosters strong relationships. We create an atmosphere of respect and authenticity when we are open and honest about our intentions, motivations, and actions.

It is also essential to seek accountability from others. Surrounding ourselves with individuals who embody humility and integrity can provide valuable support and guidance on our journey. By sharing our goals and seeking feedback, we can stay aligned with our values and ensure we remain on the right path.

Living With A Sense Of Destiny

Living with a sense of destiny means recognizing that our lives are part of a larger purpose, shaped by God's plans for us. When we understand our divine calling, we approach life with greater meaning and direction. Destiny gives us a vision of what we are meant to achieve, empowering us to pursue our goals confidently.

One of the first steps in living with a sense of destiny is to seek God's guidance. This involves prayer, meditation, and reflection on His word. By spending time in God's presence, we open ourselves up to His leading and allow Him to reveal His unique plans for us. Proverbs 3:5-6 encourages us, *"Trust in the Lord with all your heart, and lean not on your understanding; in all your ways acknowledge Him, and He shall direct your paths."*

When we acknowledge God in all our ways, we see how our daily choices align with our destiny. Each decision becomes a building block contributing to fulfilling our purpose. Living with a sense of destiny requires us to be intentional about our choices, ensuring they reflect our commitment to God's plan.

Embracing God's Vision For Your Life

Embracing God's vision for our lives means letting go of our ambitions and desires in favor of His grander plan. It requires humility to surrender our desires and trust that God knows what is best for us. Isaiah 55:8-9 reminds us, *"For My thoughts are not your thoughts, nor are your ways My ways, says the Lord. As the heavens are higher than the earth, so are My ways higher than your ways, and My thoughts than your thoughts."*

When we submit to God's vision, we align ourselves with His purposes, opening doors to opportunities we may never have considered. Often, the path God sets before us may not match our initial expectations, but it is essential to trust that He is guiding us toward something more significant.

Living with a sense of destiny also means being open to change and adaptation. God's plans may unfold differently than we anticipate, and we must remain flexible as we navigate our journeys. This flexibility allows us to embrace new opportunities and experiences contributing to our growth and success.

The Role Of Faith In Your Destiny

Faith is essential in living with a sense of destiny. It is through faith that we believe in God's promises for our lives and trust in His timing. Hebrews 11:1 defines faith as *"the substance of things hoped for, the evidence of things not seen."* Living with a sense of destiny often requires us to step out in faith, taking risks and pursuing opportunities that may seem uncertain.

When we embrace our destiny, we may face doubts and fears. However, it is essential to remember that faith does not eliminate uncertainty; it enables us to move forward despite it. By trusting in God's plan, we find the courage to take steps toward fulfilling our purpose, knowing that He is with us every step of the way.

Also, our faith encourages us to rely on God's strength rather than our own. Philippians 4:13 reminds us, *"I can do all things through Christ who strengthens me."*
When we face challenges on our journey, we can lean on Christ's strength, knowing He equips us to fulfill our destiny.

Building Community And Support

Living with a sense of destiny is not meant to be a solitary endeavor. God places people in our lives to support us and encourage us as we pursue our goals. Building a community of like-minded individuals who share our values can provide accountability, guidance, and inspiration.

As we pursue our destiny, we must seek out relationships that uplift and empower us. Surrounding ourselves with individuals who embody humility and integrity encourages us to grow and remain aligned with our values. In times of doubt or uncertainty, having a supportive community can remind us of our purpose and help us stay focused on our goals.

We should also be willing to contribute to others' success.

Supporting and uplifting those around us fosters a sense of community and reflects the principles of humility and integrity. When we celebrate the achievements of others and offer our assistance, we create a positive environment where everyone can thrive.

In conclusion, living with a sense of destiny means acknowledging that your life has a purpose and that you are part of a greater plan. Trust in God's guidance as you pursue your goals, and remain open to His leading and timing. Each step you take toward fulfilling your destiny is a testament to your commitment to God's expectations for your life.

By embracing humility, integrity, and a sense of destiny, you will find that your journey to success becomes more meaningful, purposeful, and impactful. True success is not merely about what you achieve but about who you become in the process, an individual who reflects the love and grace of God to the world.

CHAPTER FIVE

RELATIONSHIP NAVIGATION: STRATEGIES FOR SUCCESS

R elationships are vital to our lives, profoundly influencing our personal growth, success, and overall well-being. Whether in our families, friendships, workplaces, or communities, the quality of our relationships can determine the trajectory of our lives.

The Value Of Relationships

We enter a web of relationships from birth that shape our identities and experiences. Relationships provide us with support, encouragement, and a sense of belonging. They can be a source of joy and fulfillment, enhancing our lives in countless ways. Conversely, toxic or unhealthy relationships can lead to stress, dissatisfaction, and emotional turmoil.

We saw in Proverbs 27:17, "*As iron sharpens iron, so one person sharpens another.*" This verse explains the positive impact that healthy relationships can have on our growth. Engaging with others who uplift, challenge, and inspire us allows us to grow and develop meaningfully. Healthy relationships create an environment where we can learn from one another, share experiences, and support each other through life's challenges.

Moreover, our relationships significantly influence our success. Successful individuals often attribute their achievements to the support and encouragement they receive from others. Mentors, friends, and family members play a crucial role in guiding us, offering advice, and providing resources that help us navigate the complexities of life. Building healthy relationships is beneficial and essential for achieving our goals and living fulfilling lives.

Characteristics Of Healthy Relationships

To build healthy and meaningful relationships, understanding their defining characteristics is crucial.
Healthy relationships are marked by several essential qualities, reflecting the wisdom of *"Love each other as I have loved you."* (John 15:12, NIV)

Trust: The Foundation
Trust is the cornerstone of any healthy relationship.

It involves honesty, transparency, and a safe environment where both parties feel comfortable sharing thoughts, feelings, and vulnerabilities.
Trust is built over time through consistent actions and open communication.

As Proverbs 11:13 reminds us, *"Whoever goes about slandering reveals secrets, but he who is trustworthy in spirit keeps a thing covered."* (Proverbs 11:13, ESV)

Respect: Valuing Each Other
Healthy relationships are built on mutual respect.

This means valuing each other's opinions, feelings, and boundaries.

In a respectful relationship, both individuals feel heard and appreciated, even when disagreeing.
Respect ensures understanding and empathy, allowing relationships to flourish.

Communication: The Key to Understanding
Open and honest communication is essential for maintaining healthy relationships.

This involves actively listening, expressing thoughts and feelings clearly, and addressing conflicts constructively.

Good communication prevents misunderstandings and strengthens the bond between individuals.

As Ephesians 4:29 encourages, *"Do not let any unwholesome talk come out of your mouths, but only what is helpful for building others up."* (Ephesians 4:29, NIV)

Support: A Strong Safety Net
Healthy relationships provide a robust support system. This means being there for one another during challenging times, offering encouragement, and celebrating each other's successes.

Supportive relationships help individuals feel valued and connected, providing a sense of belonging.

Boundaries: Preserving Balance
Establishing healthy boundaries is crucial for maintaining balance in relationships.

Boundaries define acceptable and unacceptable behavior, helping individuals protect their emotional and physical well-being.

Healthy relationships honor each other's boundaries, promoting autonomy and respect.

Building Meaningful Relationships

Building meaningful relationships requires intentional effort and commitment. Here are some practical steps to cultivate healthy and meaningful connections:

Invest Time: Relationships require time and attention to grow. Make a conscious effort to invest time in the people you care about. This could involve setting aside regular time for family, reaching out to friends, or participating in community activities. The more time you spend with others, the stronger your connections will become.

Be Present: When spending time with others, strive to be fully present. Put away distractions such as phones or laptops, and engage in meaningful conversations. Being present shows that you value the relationship and care about the other person's thoughts and feelings.

Practice Deliberate Listening: Deliberate listening is a vital skill for building healthy relationships. It involves hearing what someone is saying and understanding their perspective. Show genuine interest in the conversation by asking questions, providing feedback, and validating their feelings. This demonstrates respect and fosters deeper connections.

Share Experiences: Shared experiences can strengthen bonds and create lasting memories. Engage in activities together, whether going for a walk, attending a concert, or participating in a community event. These shared moments provide opportunities for connection and deepen your understanding of one another.

Be Vulnerable: Vulnerability is a key component of meaningful relationships. When you share your thoughts, feelings, and struggles, you create a space for others to do the same. Being vulnerable ensures trust and intimacy, allowing relationships to grow stronger. Remember that vulnerability is not a sign of weakness; it is a courageous step toward a deeper connection.

Offer Support: Be proactive in offering support to others. Whether it's lending a listening ear, providing encouragement during difficult times, or celebrating their achievements, showing support reinforces the bond between individuals. Let others know you are there for them, and they will be more likely to reciprocate.

Seek Feedback: Healthy relationships thrive on open communication and feedback. Ask for input from those you care about to improve your relationship. Be willing to listen to their suggestions and be open to making changes. This demonstrates that you value their perspective and are committed to fostering a healthy connection.

Navigating Conflicts

No relationship is without its challenges, and conflicts are a natural part of any meaningful connection. How we handle these conflicts can significantly impact the strength of our relationships. Here are some strategies for effectively managing conflicts:

Stay Calm: When conflicts arise, it is essential to remain calm and composed. Taking a step back to collect your thoughts before responding can prevent escalation and lead to more productive conversations. Practice deep breathing or take a brief break if needed.

Focus on the Issue: During conflicts, focus on the specific issue at hand rather than making personal attacks or generalizations. Use "I" statements to express how you feel and what you need, rather than blaming the other person. For example, say "I feel hurt when..." instead of "You always..."

Seek Common Ground: Look for areas of agreement during conflicts. Finding common ground can help de-escalate tensions and create a sense of unity. Focus on solutions that benefit both parties, rather than dwelling on who is right or wrong.

Be Willing to Compromise: Compromise is often necessary in resolving conflicts. Be open to finding a middle ground that satisfies both parties. This requires flexibility and a willingness to put the relationship above personal pride.

Forgive and Move Forward: After resolving a conflict, practice forgiveness. Holding onto grudges can poison relationships and hinder personal growth. Forgiveness does not mean forgetting; it means letting go of the hurt and choosing to move forward with a renewed commitment to the relationship.

Lastly, as you navigate your relationships, remember the importance of mutual respect, healthy communication, and empathy. Invest time and effort into building connections that align with your values and contribute to your growth. Surround yourself with individuals who inspire and uplift you, and be willing to distance yourself from toxic relationships that hinder your progress.

When you embrace healthy relationships, you enhance your success and create a positive ripple effect in the lives of others. Relationships are not just an aspect of life but a vital component of our journey toward fulfillment and purpose. Embrace the value of healthy connections, and let them guide you on your path to success.

Identifying Toxic Relationships

Relationships have the potential to enrich our lives, provide support, and help us grow. However, not all relationships are positive or conducive to our well-being. Instead of uplifting us, some relationships can drain our energy, hinder our progress, and even damage our emotional, mental, and spiritual health. These are what we call toxic relationships. Identifying and managing toxic relationships is crucial to achieving success and maintaining a healthy, balanced life.

What Is A Toxic Relationship?

A toxic relationship is any relationship in which one or both parties consistently exhibit behaviors that are harmful, manipulative, or unhealthy. These relationships can occur in any context: friendships, family dynamics, romantic partnerships, or professional interactions. Patterns of control, manipulation, disrespect, and emotional harm mark toxic relationships.

While every relationship will have its challenges, what distinguishes a toxic relationship from a normal one is the frequency and intensity of negative interactions.

In a toxic relationship, these negative patterns are persistent and rarely resolved healthily. Instead of contributing to personal growth, these relationships often undermine one's confidence, self-worth, and emotional stability.

Signs Of A Toxic Relationship

Identifying a toxic relationship can be difficult, significantly, when we are emotionally invested in the relationship. However, several vital signs can help us recognize an unhealthy relationship. Below are some of the most common indicators:

Constant Criticism: In a toxic relationship, criticism goes beyond helpful feedback or constructive suggestions. Instead, it becomes a continuous tool for belittling or demeaning the other person. This criticism often targets the individual's character or identity, making them feel inadequate or unworthy. When someone consistently points out your flaws or weaknesses without offering support or encouragement, it can lead to a decline in self-esteem.

Healthy relationships, in contrast, are built on mutual respect and constructive communication. While occasional disagreements or critiques are normal, these should never be used to demean or devalue another person.

Manipulation and Control: Toxic individuals often seek to control others through manipulation. This can take many forms, such as emotional blackmail, guilt-tripping, or gaslighting, where the manipulative person tries to make you doubt your perception of reality. They may use these tactics to maintain power over you or force you to conform to their desires.

In toxic relationships, manipulation can also manifest as attempts to isolate you from others. Toxic individuals may discourage you from spending time with friends, family, or colleagues to keep you dependent on them.

Lack of Support: Healthy relationships are characterized by mutual support, where both parties encourage each other's growth and well-being. In a toxic relationship, support is often one-sided or absent. Instead of celebrating your successes, the other person may minimize your achievements or make you feel guilty for pursuing your goals.

When someone consistently undermines your dreams, refuses to acknowledge your accomplishments, or discourages your efforts, they may engage in toxic behavior. This lack of support can make you feel isolated and discouraged, preventing you from reaching your full potential.

Emotional Drain: Toxic relationships often leave you feeling emotionally exhausted, anxious, or drained. If you frequently feel stressed, upset, or on edge after interacting with someone, it may be a sign that the relationship is toxic. These relationships can create a sense of dread, as you may begin to anticipate negative interactions or conflicts whenever you engage with the person.

Healthy relationships, on the other hand, leave you feeling supported, understood, and energized. While no relationship is perfect, consistent emotional strain is a red flag that the relationship may be causing more harm than good.

Disrespect and Boundary Violations: Respect is a cornerstone of any healthy relationship. In toxic relationships, respect is often lacking, and boundaries are frequently crossed or ignored. Toxic individuals may dismiss your feelings, belittle your experiences, or act in ways that disregard your limits. For example, they may intrude on your privacy, disregard your need for personal space, or pressure you into doing things that make you uncomfortable.

When someone repeatedly violates your boundaries, it indicates a lack of respect for your autonomy and well-being. Healthy relationships honor and respect each person's boundaries, ensuring both parties feel safe and valued.

Jealousy and Possessiveness: Toxic relationships are often marked by excessive jealousy and possessiveness. The toxic individual may become overly suspicious of your interactions with others, leading to frequent accusations or controlling behaviors. They may try to monitor your actions, dictate who you can and cannot spend time with, or become hostile when you form connections with other people.

While some degree of jealousy is average in relationships, excessive jealousy, and possessiveness are signs of insecurity and control. These behaviors create an environment of fear and mistrust, making maintaining a healthy and balanced relationship challenging.

Blame and Refusal to Take Responsibility: In toxic relationships, the poisonous individual often refuses to take responsibility for their actions. Instead, they shift blame onto others, making you feel responsible for their behavior or the problems in the relationship. This pattern of blaming can create a sense of guilt and confusion, as you may question whether you are at fault for the issues in the relationship.

Healthy relationships, by contrast, involve accountability. Both parties are willing to acknowledge their mistakes, apologize when necessary, and work together to resolve conflicts.

The Impact Of Toxic Relationships On Your Success

Toxic relationships can have far-reaching consequences, affecting your emotional well-being and personal and professional success. The negative energy, stress, and emotional turmoil caused by these relationships can consume your mental and emotional resources, leaving little room for personal growth and achievement.

As Proverbs 22:24-25 cautions, *"Do not make friends with a hot-tempered person, do not associate with one easily angered, or you may learn their ways and get yourself ensnared."* (Proverbs 22:24-25, NIV)

Loss of Focus and Motivation
When you are constantly dealing with the stress and conflict of a toxic relationship, it becomes difficult to focus on your goals and ambitions.
The emotional toll of toxic relationships can drain your motivation, leaving you feeling overwhelmed or discouraged.

You may struggle to stay committed to your projects or lose interest in pursuing your dreams.

Decreased Self-Esteem
Toxic relationships often chip away at your self-esteem, leaving you doubting your abilities and worth. Constant criticism, manipulation, and disrespect can lead you to question your value and potential.

When you don't believe in yourself, taking risks, pursuing new opportunities, and asserting yourself professionally becomes more difficult.

As Psalm 139:14 reminds us, *"I praise you because I am fearfully and wonderfully made."* (Psalm 139:14, NIV)

Isolation and Reduced Support
Toxic individuals may isolate you from supportive friends, family, or colleagues, leaving you without a solid network to rely on.
This isolation can prevent you from seeking the advice, encouragement, and resources essential for personal and professional success.

A lack of support can make navigating challenges or maintaining momentum toward your goals difficult.

Emotional Burnout
The emotional strain of toxic relationships can lead to burnout.

Constant stress, anxiety, and emotional exhaustion can take a toll on your mental and physical health, making it harder to stay productive and focused.

Over time, burnout can affect work performance, ability to meet deadlines, and overall well-being.

Fear of Change and Growth
Toxic individuals often discourage growth and change, preferring to keep the relationship stagnant to maintain control.

In a toxic relationship, you may feel pressured to stay the same, even when personal growth or professional advancement requires change.
This resistance to change can prevent you from seizing new opportunities or pursuing the next step in your career.

Philippians 1:9-10 encourages, *"And this is my prayer: that your love may abound more and more in knowledge and depth of insight, so that you may be able to discern what is best."* (Philippians 1:9-10, NIV)

Breaking Free from Toxic Relationships
Recognizing that a relationship is toxic is the first step toward breaking free from its negative influence.

However, ending or distancing yourself from a toxic relationship can be challenging, especially if the relationship is long-standing or emotionally complex.

Psalm 1:1 advises, *"Blessed are those who do not follow the counsel of the wicked, or stand in the way of sinners, or sit in the seat of scoffers."* (Psalm 1:1, ESV)

Steps To Freedom

Acknowledge the Reality
It's essential to acknowledge the reality of the situation.

Denying or downplaying the toxicity of the relationship only prolongs the harm it causes.
Be honest about the relationship's negative impact on your life, emotions, and success.

Recognize that you deserve healthy, supportive relationships that contribute to your growth.
As 2 Timothy 2:22 reminds us, *"Flee the evil desires of youth and pursue righteousness, faith, love, and peace, along with those who call on the Lord out of a pure heart."* (2 Timothy 2:22, NIV)

Set Boundaries
Once you recognize that a relationship is toxic, setting boundaries is crucial in protecting yourself.

Communicate your boundaries clearly and assertively, letting the other person know what behaviors are unacceptable.

Be firm in maintaining these boundaries, even if the other person resists or attempts to manipulate you into compromising them.

Seek Support
Ending a toxic relationship can be emotionally draining, and it's essential to seek support from trusted friends, family, or a therapist.

Talking to someone who understands your situation can provide validation, guidance, and encouragement.

Surround yourself with individuals who uplift and empower you, offering a safe space to heal and grow.

As Galatians 6:2 says, *"Carry each other's burdens, and in this way, you will fulfill the law of Christ."* (Galatians 6:2, NLT)

Limit Contact or Cut Ties
Sometimes, it may be necessary to limit contact with the toxic individual or cut ties altogether.
If the relationship is causing significant harm, distance yourself physically and emotionally.

This may involve reducing communication, avoiding situations where you will interact with the person, or, in extreme cases, severing the relationship entirely.

Prioritize Self-Care
Breaking free from a toxic relationship can be emotionally challenging, so it's essential to prioritize self-care during this time.

Engage in activities that nourish your mind, body, and spirit, such as exercise, meditation, journaling, or spending time with supportive loved ones.

Self-care helps you rebuild your sense of self-worth and emotional resilience.

Focus on Personal Growth
Use the experience of leaving a toxic relationship as an opportunity for personal growth.
Reflect on your lessons and how you can apply them to future relationships.

Focus on your goals, ambitions, and well-being, and surround yourself with positive influences encouraging growth.

As Philippians 4:13 states, *"I can do all this through him who gives me strength."* (Philippians 4:13, NKJV)

Breaking Free, Embracing Fulfillment

Identifying toxic relationships is crucial for protecting your emotional well-being and success.

Toxic relationships can drain your energy, diminish your self-worth, and hinder your personal and professional progress.

By recognizing the signs of toxicity and taking steps to distance yourself from harmful individuals, you free yourself to pursue healthier, more fulfilling relationships.

Remember that you deserve relationships that uplift, support, and inspire you.

Invest your time and energy in connections that contribute to your growth, and be willing to walk away from relationships that bring harm or negativity into your life.

By surrounding yourself with healthy relationships, you create an environment where you can thrive, achieve your goals, and live a life aligned with your values and purpose.

CHAPTER SIX

KEYS TO SUSTAINING SUCCESS

Achieving success is one part of the journey, but sustaining that success is an entirely different challenge. Many reach their goals only to find that maintaining their progress and growth requires more dedication and effort. Two critical keys to sustaining success are discipline and accountability. These qualities are essential for ensuring that success is momentary and lasting, enabling individuals to continue growing, achieving, and remaining aligned with their purpose.

The Role Of Discipline In Sustaining Success

Discipline is the consistent practice of self-control, focus, and perseverance, even when challenges arise or motivation wanes. The internal drive pushes you to continue making progress, regardless of external circumstances. Discipline keeps you committed to your goals when distractions, fatigue, or temptations attempt to steer you off course. Without discipline, success becomes difficult to sustain, as it is easy to lose focus or become complacent after achieving initial milestones.

Proverbs 12:1 says, *"Whoever loves discipline loves knowledge, but whoever hates correction is stupid."* This verse shows the connection between discipline and growth. Discipline helps us remain teachable and open to correction, allowing us to improve and move forward continuously.

Consistency is Key

One of the most important aspects of discipline is consistency. Consistency in your actions, habits, and efforts creates momentum. You build a foundation for long-term success when you consistently work toward your goals, even in small ways. Consistency prevents stagnation and ensures that you always move closer to your objectives.

Consider the story of athletes who train for years to reach peak performance. They do not rely on sporadic bursts of effort but follow a disciplined daily practice routine, honing their skills and building endurance over time. Similarly, in any field, whether it's business, education, or personal development, consistency is the engine that drives sustained success.

Philippians 3:14 encourages us to *"press on toward the goal to win the prize for which God has called [us]."* This scripture reminds us of the importance of persistence and continuous effort. Success is not a one-time achievement but a journey that requires ongoing discipline and perseverance.

The Power of Habits

Discipline is often built through the cultivation of good habits. Habits are the small, consistent actions we take every day that contribute to our long-term success. Developing positive habits, such as time management, goal-setting, and regular self-reflection, allows us to stay on track and focus on what truly matters.

For example, a successful entrepreneur might develop the habit of reviewing their business strategies every morning, setting daily goals, and checking in with their team regularly. Over time, these habits create a structure that supports the sustainability of their success. Likewise, in your personal or professional life, identifying and cultivating habits that align with your goals can help you maintain discipline and progress toward your vision.

Building and maintaining good habits also requires intentional effort. It is essential to know which habits contribute to or detract from your success. Reflect on your daily routines and identify areas where you can make minor improvements. Doing this creates a disciplined lifestyle that fosters growth and success.

Overcoming Obstacles with Discipline

Life consists of obstacles, unexpected challenges, setbacks, and distractions that can derail our progress without discipline. However, discipline gives us the strength to overcome these obstacles and stay focused on our goals.

When faced with adversity, losing motivation or feeling discouraged is easy. Yet, discipline teaches us to push through difficult times, trusting that perseverance will lead to eventual success. James 1:12 reminds us, *"Blessed is the one who perseveres under trial because, having stood the test, that person will receive the crown of life that the Lord has promised."* Discipline equips us to stand firm in trials, knowing that our effort and endurance will be rewarded.

For example, consider someone trying to build a successful career. They may face rejection, criticism, or financial difficulties along the way. However, if they remain disciplined, continue to work hard, improve their skills, and seek new opportunities, they increase their chances of overcoming those challenges and ultimately achieving lasting success.

Discipline is also essential for managing distractions. It can be easy to lose focus in a world full of social media, entertainment, and endless demands on our time. Discipline allows us to prioritize our goals and limit distractions, ensuring we stay on the path to success. By setting clear boundaries and committing to our priorities, we safeguard our time and energy for the things that truly matter.

Accountability As A Tool For Sustained Success

While discipline is essentially an internal practice, accountability involves external support. Accountability is holding yourself responsible for your actions and decisions while allowing others to provide feedback, guidance, and encouragement. It helps ensure you stay true to your goals, even when facing challenges or distractions.

Surrounding yourself with individuals who support your journey can provide the motivation and structure needed to maintain success. Accountability encourages us to remain committed to our goals, offering a system of checks and balances that keeps us aligned with our values and vision.

Building an Accountability Network
An accountability network consists of individuals like friends, mentors, colleagues, or even coaches who help you stay on track by offering support, encouragement, and constructive feedback. These individuals are invested in your success and are willing to hold you accountable for the goals you set for yourself.

Building an accountability network begins by identifying people who share your values and are committed to your growth. These individuals should be trustworthy and able to provide honest feedback without judgment. They should also be willing to challenge you when necessary, pushing you to reach your full potential.

For example, a business owner might create an accountability network by forming a group of fellow entrepreneurs who meet regularly to discuss their goals, challenges, and progress. By sharing their experiences and receiving feedback from others, they gain new perspectives and stay motivated to continue pursuing their vision.

Accountability can also be found in personal relationships. A close friend or family member can be an accountability partner, helping you stay true to your commitments and offering encouragement when facing difficulties. Having someone to check in with regularly helps reinforce discipline and keeps you focused on your long-term objectives.

Accountability to God
While accountability to others is necessary, it is also essential to maintain accountability to God. As believers, our ultimate goal is to align our lives with His will and purpose.

We are accountable to God for how we use the gifts, talents, and opportunities He has given us. By seeking His guidance through prayer and reflection, we ensure that our actions and decisions align with His life plan.

Romans 14:12 reminds us, "*So then, each of us will give an account of ourselves to God.*" This verse emphasizes the importance of personal responsibility and accountability in our relationship with God. As we pursue success, it is vital to regularly assess whether our efforts are aligned with God's expectations and whether we are using our success to glorify Him.

Maintaining accountability to God also involves being honest about our intentions and motivations. Are we pursuing success for selfish reasons, or are we using our success to serve others and honor God? Regularly reflecting on these questions ensures that our success is sustainable and rooted in integrity and purpose.

Benefits of Accountability
Accountability offers several benefits that contribute to success's sustainability. First, it helps prevent complacency. When we achieve a certain level of success, it is easy to become comfortable and stop pushing ourselves to grow. However, accountability partners can challenge us to continue striving for excellence even after we've reached our goals.

Secondly, accountability provides support during difficult times.

When we face setbacks or challenges, having people who can offer encouragement and guidance is helpful. They can remind us of our goals and help us stay motivated, even when discouraged.

Thirdly, accountability promotes personal growth. Receiving feedback from others gives us new insights into our strengths and weaknesses. This feedback helps us identify areas for improvement and refine our approach to achieving success. We are constantly learning and evolving through accountability, essential for sustained success.

Finally, accountability creates a sense of community. Success is rarely achieved in isolation, often involving collaboration and support from others. By building an accountability network, we form meaningful connections with individuals who share our values and are invested in our growth. These relationships provide a strong foundation for continued success.

Developing Self-Accountability
While external accountability is essential, self-accountability is equally crucial for sustaining success. Self-accountability involves taking responsibility for your actions, decisions, and progress. It requires you to be honest about your efforts, regularly assess your progress, and hold yourself to high standards.

Developing self-accountability begins with setting clear, measurable goals and tracking your progress. Whether through journaling, creating a checklist, or using an app, regularly monitoring your progress helps you stay focused and committed to your goals.

Self-accountability also involves practicing self-discipline. This means setting boundaries, staying organized, and prioritizing your time effectively. You create a disciplined lifestyle that supports long-term success by holding yourself accountable for your daily habits and actions.

Discipline and accountability are the cornerstones of sustained success. Discipline provides the internal drive to remain focused, consistent, and resilient in facing challenges. It ensures that we continue to grow and progress toward our goals, even when motivation fades. Conversely, accountability offers external support and guidance, helping us stay on track and providing feedback that fosters personal growth.

If we can develop both discipline and accountability in our lives, we create a strong foundation for lasting success. We remain committed to our goals, continuously learn and improve, and surround ourselves with individuals who encourage our growth. As we pursue our vision, let us remember that true success is not a destination but a journey of consistent effort, self-reflection, and accountability to ourselves, others, and God.

The Role Of Wisdom And Diligence

As we strive for success, we often focus on setting goals, developing discipline, and building accountability. However, wisdom and diligence are two essential keys that can significantly enhance our ability to sustain success.

While discipline keeps us on track, wisdom helps us make informed decisions, and diligence empowers us to consistently put in the necessary effort. These qualities create a powerful combination that can lead to enduring success in our lives.

Wisdom is the ability to make sound judgments and decisions based on knowledge, experience, and discernment. It goes beyond mere intelligence or the accumulation of facts; wisdom involves understanding the more profound implications of our choices and the ability to apply our knowledge in practical ways.

In Proverbs 4:7, we are told, "*Wisdom is the principal thing; therefore, get wisdom. And in all, you're getting, get understanding.*" This verse emphasizes the importance of seeking wisdom as a foundational aspect of a successful life.

Wisdom allows us to handle complexities and uncertainties,

providing clarity in moments of confusion. It helps us consider the long-term consequences of our decisions rather than being swayed by immediate gratification. Wisdom encourages us to step back, evaluate our options, and seek guidance from God and trusted advisors.

The Sources Of Wisdom

The pursuit of wisdom begins with a commitment to learning and growth. We can cultivate wisdom through various sources.

Scripture: Divine Guidance
The Bible is a treasure trove of wisdom.
"If any of you lacks wisdom, let him ask of God, who gives to all liberally and without reproach, and it will be given to him." (James 1:5, NKJV) reminds us that Scripture offers insights into life's challenging relationships and decision-making.
Regular study and prayerful seeking of God's guidance deepen our understanding of His will and principles.

Life Experiences: Lessons Learned
Our life experiences—successes and failures—are invaluable teachers.

Reflecting on past decisions and outcomes allows us to gain insight into our choices. We learn valuable lessons from mistakes, enabling better decision-making in the future.

Mentorship: Sharpening Minds
Seeking guidance from mentors or wise individuals provides valuable perspectives.
Proverbs 27:17 states, *"As iron sharpens iron, so one person sharpens another."* (Proverbs 27:17, NIV)

Mentors share experiences, offer advice, and help navigate challenges.

Education: Intellectual Growth

Formal education and training contribute to our wisdom. Acquired knowledge and skills enable informed decision-making in personal and professional lives. Continuous learning fosters intellectual growth and critical thinking.

Applying Wisdom to Decision-Making

Wisdom is most effective when applied to our decision-making processes. In our pursuit of success, we often face numerous choices that can significantly impact our lives. Applying wisdom in decision-making involves several key steps:

Gather Information: Before deciding, gather relevant information and assess the situation. Consider the facts, evaluate your options, and seek insights from trusted sources. This information-gathering phase allows you to make informed decisions rather than relying on impulse or emotion.

Seek God's Guidance: In prayer, seek God's wisdom and discernment. Ask for clarity and understanding, trusting He will guide your decisions. Matthew 7:7 reminds us to ask, seek, and knock, knowing that God desires to guide us in our choices.

Consider the Consequences: Before committing to a decision, reflect on the potential positive and negative consequences. How will your choice impact your long-term goals? Will it align with your values and purpose? By considering the implications, you can make decisions that lead to sustainable success.

Learn from Others: Look to the experiences of others who have faced similar decisions. What lessons can you learn from their successes and mistakes? By learning from the experiences of others, you can avoid common pitfalls and make wiser choices.

Trust Your Instincts: While gathering information and seeking guidance is essential, don't underestimate your intuition. Our instincts can often provide valuable insights. If something doesn't feel right, take time to reassess before proceeding.

Be Willing to Adapt: Life is unpredictable, and sometimes, our decisions may not yield the expected outcomes. When this happens, be willing to reassess and adapt. Wisdom involves recognizing when to adjust your course and seek new growth opportunities.

The Importance Of Diligence

Diligence is being hardworking, persistent, and dedicated to completing tasks with care and attention to detail. It is the consistent effort and determination required to achieve our goals. Diligence is essential in sustaining success, as it enables us to remain committed to our pursuits, even in the face of obstacles.

Proverbs 13:4 says, "*The soul of a lazy man desires, and has nothing; but the soul of the diligent shall be made rich.*" This verse highlights the contrast between laziness and diligence, emphasizing that hard work and dedication lead to rewards and success.

The Characteristics Of Diligence

Diligence encompasses several key characteristics that contribute to sustained success:

Consistency: Diligence involves consistently putting in the effort required to achieve our goals. This means establishing routines and habits aligning with our objectives and committing to them daily. Consistency creates momentum and fosters growth.

Commitment: Diligence requires a deep commitment to our goals. It involves a willingness to persevere through challenges, setbacks, and disappointments. When genuinely committed, we are more likely to stay focused and work hard, even when the journey gets tough.

Attention to Detail: Diligence involves paying attention to details and ensuring our work is of high quality. This commitment to excellence sets us apart and demonstrates our dedication to our pursuits. When we put in the effort to ensure our work is thorough and accurate, we build a reputation for reliability and professionalism.

Resilience: Diligence is characterized by the ability to bounce back from failures and setbacks. Those who are diligent understand that obstacles are a natural part of the journey and are willing to learn from their experiences rather than give up. Resilience helps us maintain a positive attitude and continue striving for our goals.

Time Management: Diligence also involves effective time management. Being diligent means prioritizing tasks, setting deadlines, and staying organized. By managing our time wisely, we can maximize our productivity and consistently progress toward our goals.

The Path Of Diligence

To build diligence in your life, consider the following strategies, guided by the wisdom of Proverbs 22:29, *"Do you see someone skilled in their work? They will serve before kings; they will not serve before officials of low rank."* (Proverbs 22:29, NIV)

Set Clear Goals
Establish clear, achievable goals that provide direction for your efforts. A clear target enables focused energy and resource allocation. Break larger goals into smaller, manageable steps for a more approachable journey.

Create a Routine
Develop a daily routine that incorporates actions required to achieve your goals. Routines provide structure and establish discipline and commitment to objectives.

As Psalm 90:12 reminds us, *"Teach us to number our days, that we may gain a heart of wisdom."* (Psalm 90:12, NKJV)

Eliminate Distractions
Identify and eliminate distractions hindering focus and diligence.

Set technology boundaries, create a dedicated workspace, or minimize interruptions.

Stay Organized
Organize tasks and priorities using to-do lists, planners, or digital apps. Organization enhances efficiency and maintains focus.

Celebrate Progress
Acknowledge and celebrate progress along the way. Recognizing achievements reinforces motivation and commitment to continued diligence.

Celebrating milestones maintains high spirits and reminds you of the journey's purpose.

Stay Accountable
Share goals with someone who can hold you accountable. A mentor, friend, or accountability partner encourages commitment and diligence.
Galatians 6:2 advises, *"Carry each other's burdens, and in this way, you will fulfill the law of Christ."* (Galatians 6:2, NLT)

Balancing Wisdom And Diligence

Wisdom and diligence are powerful qualities that work best together. Wisdom offers the insights and guidance necessary for making informed decisions, while diligence ensures that we consistently work to follow through on those decisions.

For example, applying wisdom helps you assess the risks, gather necessary information, and develop a solid plan when embarking on a new project. Once the plan is in place, diligence empowers you to execute it with determination and persistence.

Striking a balance between wisdom and diligence involves regularly reflecting on your progress and adjusting your approach as needed. Seek opportunities for learning and growth, and remain open to feedback that can enhance your understanding and effectiveness.

Wisdom and diligence are essential keys to sustaining success. Wisdom guides our decision-making processes, helping us handle complexities and make informed choices. Diligence fuels our efforts, ensuring that we remain committed to our goals and put in the necessary work to achieve them.

As you continue on your journey toward success, prioritize cultivating wisdom and diligence in your life. Seek knowledge, learn from experiences, and apply your insights to decision-making. Embrace the power of diligence by committing to consistent effort and hard work.

By embodying these qualities, you position yourself for sustained success and create a life filled with purpose and fulfillment. True success is not just about reaching goals; it is about becoming the person God created you to be and living in alignment with His plan for your life.

Cultivating Godly Relationships

As we journey through life and pursue our goals, the relationships we build play a pivotal role in our success. Healthy, supportive relationships enhance our well-being and provide the encouragement and accountability needed to overcome challenges.

Cultivating godly relationships is essential for sustaining success. These relationships are characterized by mutual respect, love, and a shared commitment to align with God's will. This section will explore the importance of cultivating godly relationships and how they contribute to our overall success and fulfillment.

The Foundation Of Godly Relationships

Godly relationships are built on shared values, faith, and mutual respect. These relationships reflect the love of Christ and are characterized by qualities such as honesty, integrity, empathy, and support. Engaging in relationships that honor God creates an environment conducive to growth, healing, and success.

Shared Faith: A godly relationship begins with a shared faith in Christ. When both individuals are rooted in their faith, they can spiritually encourage and uplift one another. This shared commitment to God creates a sense of unity and purpose, allowing both parties to grow together in their walk with Christ.

Mutual Respect: Respect is the basis of any healthy relationship. In godly relationships, both individuals value each other's opinions, feelings, and boundaries. This mutual respect creates a safe space where both parties can express themselves freely without fear of judgment or criticism.

Support and Encouragement: Godly relationships are marked by a spirit of support and encouragement. Individuals in these relationships genuinely invest in each other's growth and well-being. They celebrate each other's successes, offer comfort during challenges, and motivate each other to keep moving forward.

Commitment to Growth: Having godly relationships requires a commitment to personal and relational growth. Both individuals should be willing to invest time and effort into the relationship, seeking to deepen their understanding of one another and nurture their bond.

The Impact of Godly Relationships on Success
Godly relationships profoundly influence our success in various aspects of life. Several ways cultivating these relationships contribute to sustained success:

Accountability: In godly relationships, accountability is a vital element. Having friends or mentors who hold you accountable encourages you to stay committed to your goals and values. They can provide constructive feedback, help you stay focused, and offer support when you face challenges. Proverbs 27:17 states, *"As iron sharpens iron, so one person sharpens another.*" This mutual accountability ensures personal growth and helps you align with your goals.

Emotional Support: The journey to success can be fraught with difficulties, setbacks, and moments of self-doubt. Godly relationships provide a robust support system that helps us navigate these challenges. When we face struggles, having someone to lean on can make all the difference. A listening ear, comforting words, or shared prayer can provide the emotional support we need to persevere. Ecclesiastes 4:9-10 reminds us of the importance of companionship: "*Two are better than one because they have a good reward for their labor. For if they fall, one will lift his companion.*"

Inspiration and Motivation: Surrounding ourselves with individuals who share our values and aspirations inspires us to strive for greatness. Godly relationships expose us to new ideas, perspectives, and opportunities for growth. The encouragement we receive from others fuels our motivation and helps us overcome obstacles. We are inspired to do the same when we witness others pursuing their goals passionately and purposefully.

Shared Wisdom: Engaging with others in godly relationships allows us to benefit from their wisdom and experiences. We can learn from their successes and failures, gaining insights to guide our journey. Proverbs 19:20 encourages us to "*Listen to counsel and receive instruction, that you may be wise in your latter days.*" Seeking advice from those who have gone through similar challenges can provide valuable guidance and help us make informed decisions.

Building a Supportive Community: Building godly relationships creates a supportive community beyond individual connections. This community fosters an environment of love, encouragement, and mutual support. In times of need, a strong community can rally together to provide assistance, prayer, and encouragement.

Being part of a supportive community enhances our sense of belonging and helps us feel valued and understood.

Characteristics Of Godly Relationships

To build godly relationships, it is essential to embody specific characteristics that reflect the nature of Christ. Here are some important qualities to develop:

Love and Compassion: Love is the foundation of all godly relationships. Ephesians 4:2 encourages us to "*Be completely humble and gentle; be patient, bearing with one another in love.*" Developing an attitude of compassion and understanding creates a nurturing environment where both individuals feel valued and respected.

Honesty and Transparency: Godly relationships thrive on openness and transparency. Being open about your feelings, thoughts, and struggles fosters trust and deepens individual connections. Honesty allows for meaningful conversations and encourages vulnerability, strengthening the bond in the relationship.

Forgiveness: No relationship is perfect, and conflicts will arise. Practicing forgiveness is essential for maintaining godly relationships. Holding onto grudges or past mistakes can create barriers and hinder growth. Ephesians 4:32 reminds us to "*Be kind and compassionate to one another, forgiving each other, just as in Christ God forgave you.*" Forgiveness restores harmony and allows the relationship to move forward.

Patience: Building godly relationships requires patience, especially when handling challenges or conflicts. Recognizing that growth takes time and individuals may not always respond as we hope fosters understanding. Patience allows us to extend grace to one another and promotes collaboration.

Encouragement: Actively encouraging one another is a

vital component of godly relationships. Whether celebrating achievements, reassuring during tough times, or motivating each other to pursue goals, encouragement strengthens the bond and fosters growth. Romans 15:2 encourages us to *"Each of us should please our neighbors for their good, to build them up."*

Building Godly Relationships in Various Contexts

Godly relationships can be cultivated in various contexts, including family, friendships, and professional environments. Below are some practical steps for nurturing these relationships:

Family Relationships: Building godly relationships within families requires open communication, love, and understanding. Establish regular family gatherings where everyone can share their thoughts, experiences, and challenges. Create an environment of support and encouragement, emphasizing the importance of unity and love.

Friendships: Choose friendships that align with your values and faith. Seek out individuals who inspire you, challenge you to grow, and support your journey. Engage in activities encouraging growth and strengthening your bond, such as prayer, study groups, or volunteering.

Professional Relationships: Cultivating godly relationships in the workplace involves promoting a culture of respect and collaboration. Practice integrity and honesty in all interactions, and seek to support and uplift your colleagues. Encourage healthy communication and be willing to lend a helping hand when needed.

Community Involvement: Engaging in your community provides opportunities to cultivate godly relationships with others with similar values. Participate in local organizations, volunteer activities, or church groups. Building relationships within the community fosters a sense of belonging and creates a network of support.

Overcoming Barriers To Godly Relationships

While building godly relationships is essential, it can also be challenging. Various barriers may arise that hinder the development of these connections. There are some common obstacles and how to overcome them:

Busy Schedules: In our fast-paced lives, finding time to invest in relationships can be difficult. However, it is crucial to prioritize relationships and make intentional efforts to connect. Set aside time for family gatherings, coffee with friends, or community involvement. When relationships are a priority, we find ways to make them work.

Miscommunication: Misunderstandings and miscommunication can create tension in relationships. To overcome this barrier, practice active listening and clarify any uncertainties. Don't assume you know what the other person means; instead, ask questions and seek clarification to foster understanding.

Fear of Vulnerability: Some individuals may struggle with vulnerability, fearing rejection or judgment. Remember that healthy relationships thrive on openness and honesty. Take small steps toward vulnerability by gradually sharing your thoughts and feelings. As you build trust, it will become easier to open up.

Negative Past Experiences: Previous experiences with toxic relationships can create barriers to building new connections. Acknowledge your past, but do not allow it to define your future. Approach new relationships with a fresh perspective, understanding that not everyone will replicate the negative experiences of the past.

Lack of Support: Sometimes, we may encounter individuals who do not understand or support our desire for godly relationships. Surround yourself with a supportive community that values healthy connections. Seek mentors and like-minded individuals who can encourage you to pursue godly relationships.

Building godly relationships is a vital key to sustaining success. These relationships provide support, encouragement, and accountability, helping us handle the challenges of life and stay aligned with our purpose. By building connections rooted in shared faith, respect, and mutual support, we create an environment conducive to growth and fulfillment.

True success is not achieved in isolation, it is a journey best traveled with others. Embrace the power of godly relationships, and let them guide you toward a life of purpose, fulfillment, and lasting success.

CHAPTER SEVEN

LIVING A LIFE OF OBEDIENCE

L iving a life of obedience is a central theme in the Bible. It is aligning our actions, thoughts, and intentions with God's commands and guidance.

Obedience is not merely a set of rules to follow; it is a pathway to experiencing God's blessings, favor, and ultimate success.

The Heart Of Obedience

In the context of our faith, obedience is the act of submitting to God's authority and following His instructions. It stems from a relationship of love and trust in God, recognizing that His ways are higher than ours.

John 14:15 emphasizes this relationship: *"If you love Me, keep My commandments."* (John 14:15, NKJV)

Faithful obedience flows from love for God, highlighting the intimate connection between our willingness to obey and our relationship with Him.

The Spiritual Significance of Obedience
Obedience has significant spiritual implications.
When we choose to obey God, we demonstrate our faith and trust

in His plan for our lives.

It shows that we believe He knows what is best for us and that we are willing to follow His guidance, even when we do not fully understand the path ahead.

Aligning with God's Will

Obedience helps us align our lives with God's will.

When we follow His commands, we position ourselves to receive His guidance and blessings.

Isaiah 48:17 says, *"Thus says the Lord, your Redeemer, the Holy One of Israel: I am the Lord your God, who teaches you to profit, who leads you in the way you should go."* (Isaiah 48:17, NIV)

Having a Heart of Submission

Living a life of obedience creates a heart of submission to God. It requires humility and the recognition that we do not have all the answers.

When we submit our desires to God, we invite Him to take control of our lives.

This posture of submission creates space for Him to work in and through us, guiding us toward our divine purpose.

Experiencing God's Blessings

Obedience is often linked to experiencing God's blessings. In Deuteronomy 28:1-2, we see that obedience results in blessings: *"Now it shall come to pass, if you diligently obey the voice of the Lord your God, to observe all His commandments... that all these blessings shall come upon you and overtake you."* (Deuteronomy 28:1-2, NKJV)

The Relationship Between Obedience And Success

The relationship between obedience and success is profound. When we choose to live in obedience to God's commands, we set ourselves up for success in several key ways:

Clarity of Purpose: Obedience to God provides clarity of purpose.

When we seek to align our lives with His will, we gain insight into our unique calling and the path we are meant to follow. This clarity helps us make informed decisions and prioritize our actions toward achieving our goals. Proverbs 3:5-6 encourages us to *"Trust in the Lord with all your heart, and lean not on your own understanding; in all your ways acknowledge Him, and He shall direct your paths."* Trusting in God's guidance leads to a clear understanding of our purpose and direction.

Strengthening Character: Living a life of obedience helps shape our character and integrity. As we consistently follow God's commands, we develop qualities such as honesty, humility, and resilience. These characteristics are essential for achieving success in any area of life. When we grow strong character, we gain the trust and respect of others, opening doors to new opportunities and collaborations.

Building Trust and Credibility: Obedience enhances our credibility and reputation. When we consistently act in accordance with our values and commitments, we build trust with others.

People are more likely to support and collaborate with those who demonstrate integrity and reliability. In professional settings, obedience to ethical standards and company policies fosters a positive work environment and enhances teamwork.

Overcoming Obstacles: Life is filled with obstacles, but a life of obedience equips us to overcome challenges. When we remain obedient to God's guidance, we can face difficulties with confidence and resilience. God promises to be with us through trials, offering strength and support as we navigate the storms of life.

Romans 8:28 reassures us that *"All things work together for good to those who love God, to those who are the called according to His purpose."* This assurance gives us the confidence to persevere in obedience, knowing that God is working on our behalf.

Attracting Divine Favor: Obedience attracts God's favor into our lives. When we follow His commands and seek to honor Him in our actions, we align ourselves with His blessings. God delights in those who walk obediently and rewards them with His favor. Psalm 84:11 reminds us, *"For the Lord God is a sun and shield; the Lord will give grace and glory; no good thing will He withhold from those who walk uprightly*." This promise of divine favor is a powerful motivation to live a life of obedience.

Obedience In Everyday Life

Living a life of obedience is not limited to spiritual matters; it extends into every area of our lives. Let's see some practical ways to incorporate obedience into our daily routines:

Prioritizing Time with God: To live in obedience, we must first understand God's will for our lives. Prioritize time for prayer, Bible study, and reflection. Seek His guidance for your decisions, and listen for His voice daily. Spending time in God's presence cultivates a deeper understanding of His commands and the desires of your heart.

They are making Choices Aligned with God's Word: Our decisions should be rooted in biblical principles. Evaluate your choices against the teachings of Scripture. Ask yourself whether your actions align with God's commands and values. When faced with dilemmas, seek God's wisdom to navigate choices that honor Him.

Seeking Counsel from Others: Involve trusted mentors, friends, or spiritual leaders in decision-making. Surrounding yourself with wise individuals who share your faith can provide valuable insights and guidance. Proverbs 15:22 states, *"Without counsel, plans go awry, but in the multitude of counselors, they are established*." Seek counsel to ensure your choices are in line with God's will.

Embracing Accountability: Establish relationships that promote accountability in your spiritual walk. Share your goals and commitments with trusted friends who can encourage you and hold you accountable. This accountability fosters discipline and strengthens your commitment to obedience.

Practicing Patience: Obedience often requires patience, especially when waiting for God's timing. Trust in God's plan, even when progress feels slow. Psalm 27:14 reminds us, *"Wait on the Lord; be of good courage, and He shall strengthen your heart; wait, I say, on the Lord."* Patience is essential to obedience, allowing us to trust God's perfect timing.

The Power Of Obedience

Living a life of obedience impacts our success and transforms our hearts and minds. It deepens our relationship with God and aligns our desires with His will. As we choose to obey Him, we experience personal growth, spiritual maturity, and a profound sense of fulfillment.

Spiritual Growth: Obedience leads to spiritual growth and transformation. We develop a deeper understanding of His character and purpose as we align our lives with God's will. We learn to trust Him more fully, grow in faith, and rely on His guidance.

Strengthening Relationships: Obedience impacts our relationships with others. When we practice love, kindness, and humility, we cultivate healthy connections with those around us. Our obedience to God's commands creates an environment of mutual respect and understanding, enhancing our relationships with family, friends, and colleagues.

Establishing a Legacy of Faith: Living a life of obedience creates a legacy that reflects God's goodness and faithfulness. When others observe our commitment to obedience, they are inspired to seek a similar relationship with God. Our example can have a ripple effect, encouraging others to live according to God's will and pursue their success.

Experiencing True Fulfillment: Lastly, living a life of obedience leads to true fulfillment. When we follow God's path, we discover our purpose and experience a sense of peace that transcends worldly achievements. Success becomes not just about what we accomplish but about living a life that honors God and fulfills His plan for us.

Building A Lifestyle Of Prayer And Gratitude

A life of obedience to God is deeply intertwined with the practice of prayer and gratitude. These two elements are foundational pillars that strengthen our relationship with God, deepen our faith, and empower us to live in alignment with His will. Building a lifestyle of prayer and gratitude enhances our spiritual journey and significantly impacts our overall success and fulfillment.

The Importance Of Prayer

Prayer is a powerful means of communication with God. It is an essential component of our relationship with Him, allowing us to express our thoughts, feelings, and desires while seeking His guidance and wisdom. Through prayer, we connect with God, seeking His presence and inviting Him into our lives.

Prayer as a Source of Guidance: One of the primary purposes of prayer is to seek God's guidance in our lives. Prayer allows us to pause and reflect when we face decisions, challenges, or uncertainties. Philippians 4:6-7 encourages us: *"Be anxious for nothing, but in everything by prayer and supplication, with thanksgiving, let your requests be made known to God; and the peace of God, which surpasses all understanding, will guard your hearts and minds through Christ Jesus."* This scripture highlights the importance of bringing our concerns to God in prayer and trusting in His guidance.

Prayer Strengthens Our Faith: Regular prayer deepens our faith and reliance on God. As we communicate with Him, we develop a greater understanding of His character and His promises. Over time, our trust in God grows more robust, empowering us to face challenges confidently. When we experience God's faithfulness through answered prayers, our faith is reinforced, enabling us to step boldly into the future He has planned for us.

Prayer Ensures Intimacy with God: Just as communication is essential for any relationship, prayer nurtures our intimacy with God. When we take the time to pray, we create space for Him in our lives. We can share our joys, struggles, and desires; in return, we can listen for His voice and guidance. This intimate connection deepens our relationship with Him, allowing us to experience His love and grace fully.

Prayer Enables Transformation: Prayer is not just about seeking help or guidance but also a means of personal transformation. Through prayer, we open our hearts to God's work. As we seek His presence and guidance, we become more attuned to His desires. This transformation allows us to align our actions with His will and empowers us to live out our purpose more effectively.

Developing A Prayer Lifestyle

Building a lifestyle of prayer requires intentionality and commitment. Here are some practical steps to help you develop a consistent prayer life:

Establish a Routine: Set aside dedicated time for prayer each day. This could be in the morning, during lunch, or before bedtime. Establishing a routine helps create a habit of prayer, making it a natural part of your daily life.

Create a Prayer Space: Designate a specific space for prayer where you can focus and connect with God. This could be a quiet corner in your home, a garden, or a place where you feel at peace.

95

Having a designated space helps create an atmosphere conducive to prayer.

Use a Prayer Journal: Keeping a prayer journal can help you articulate your thoughts, feelings, and requests to God. Write down your prayers, reflections, and any insights you receive during your prayer time. This practice provides clarity and allows you to track how God works in your life.

Incorporate Scripture into Prayer: Integrating Scripture into your prayers enhances your connection with God. Use verses that resonate with your current situation or reflect your desires. Praying through Scripture helps align your heart with God's Word and deepens your understanding of His promises.

Pray in Community: Engage in prayer with others, whether through small groups, church gatherings, or prayer partners. Praying with others ensures accountability, support, and a sense of unity. It also allows you to share your burdens and joys, strengthening your relationships with fellow believers.

Be Honest and Vulnerable: Approach prayer with honesty and vulnerability. Share your struggles, doubts, and fears with God. He desires authenticity in our relationship and welcomes our honesty. When we lay bare our hearts before Him, we create space for healing and growth.

Practice Listening: Prayer is not solely about speaking; it also involves listening. After sharing your thoughts and requests, be still and listen for God's voice. He may speak to you through a sense of peace, Scripture, or insights that come to mind. Developing a listening posture enhances your ability to discern His guidance.

Make Prayer a Lifestyle: Rather than viewing prayer as a specific activity, embrace it as a lifestyle. Seek opportunities to pray throughout your day, whether it's thanking God for blessings, asking for guidance in decision-making, or interceding for others.

This ongoing dialogue with God nurtures a deeper relationship and keeps you connected to His presence.

The Power Of Gratitude

Gratitude is another essential component of sustaining success. It is the practice of recognizing and appreciating the blessings in our lives, regardless of our circumstances. Gratitude shifts our focus from what we lack to what we have, fostering a positive mindset that enhances our overall well-being.

Gratitude Brings Joy: Practicing gratitude has a powerful impact on our emotions. It encourages us to celebrate the good in our lives, even during challenging times. When we intentionally focus on the blessings, big and small, we develop a sense of joy and contentment. Philippians 4:4 tells us, "*Rejoice in the Lord always. Again, I will say, rejoice!*" Gratitude invites joy into our hearts and enables us to maintain a positive outlook.

Gratitude Strengthens Resilience: In the face of adversity, embracing gratitude helps us build resilience. By recognizing the blessings we have, we are better equipped to handle challenges with a hopeful attitude. This perspective shift allows us to approach difficulties with courage, knowing that God is with us through every trial.

Gratitude Promotes Connection: Expressing gratitude enhances our relationships with others. When we take the time to acknowledge and appreciate the people in our lives, we strengthen our bonds. Gratitude encourages us to express appreciation, creating an environment of love and support. Ephesians 5:20 encourages us to "*give thanks always for all things to God the Father in the name of our Lord Jesus Christ.*"

Gratitude Aligns Our Hearts with God: Gratitude is an acknowledgment of God's goodness and faithfulness. When we express gratitude to God, we recognize His role in our lives and acknowledge that every good gift comes from Him. This awareness deepens our relationship with God, drawing us closer to Him as we cultivate an attitude of thankfulness.

The Interconnectedness Of Prayer And Gratitude

Prayer and gratitude are interconnected practices that reinforce each other. When we engage in prayer, we often find ourselves expressing gratitude for God's blessings and faithfulness. On the other hand, building a lifestyle of gratitude leads us to a deeper desire for prayer, as we seek to connect with the God who provides for us.

Gratitude in Prayer: As we pray, we can incorporate expressions of gratitude. Thank God for specific blessings, answered prayers, and His presence in our lives. This acknowledgment of His goodness cultivates a spirit of thankfulness and draws us closer to Him.

Prayer as a Response to Gratitude: When we experience gratitude, we are often prompted to pray. Gratitude inspires us to worship and honor God, recognizing His role in our lives. This response deepens our relationship with Him and strengthens our commitment to obedience.

Mutual Reinforcement: As we develop a lifestyle of prayer and gratitude, we create a positive cycle of spiritual growth. Regular prayer helps us recognize the blessings in our lives, while gratitude enhances our motivation to engage in prayer. This mutual reinforcement ensures a deeper connection with God and enriches our overall spiritual journey.

The Transformative Power Of Prayer And Gratitude

The combination of prayer and gratitude has the power to transform our lives. When we make these practices a priority, we align our hearts with God's will and open ourselves up to His guidance and blessings.

Transforming Mindsets: Regular prayer and gratitude practices help us cultivate a positive mindset. Instead of dwelling on negativity or challenges, we shift our focus to God's goodness and the blessings He provides. This transformation allows us to approach life with hope and resilience.

Enhancing Spiritual Growth: Engaging in prayer and expressing gratitude ensures spiritual growth. We become more attuned to God's voice, recognize His work in our lives, and develop a deeper understanding of His character. This growth strengthens our faith and equips us to navigate life's challenges.

Encouraging a Community of Faith: A lifestyle of prayer and gratitude creates a sense of community among believers. When we gather to pray and express gratitude, we create an atmosphere of support and encouragement. This communal practice deepens our connections with others and reinforces our commitment to living in obedience to God.

Deepening Our Relationship with God: Finally, building a lifestyle of prayer and gratitude deepens our relationship with God. These practices draw us closer to Him, allowing us to experience His love, grace, and guidance in profound ways. As we develop intimacy with God, we are better equipped to live in obedience and fulfill His purposes for our lives.

Building a lifestyle of prayer and gratitude is essential for living a life of obedience. These practices strengthen our relationship with God, enhance our spiritual growth, and empower us to navigate the challenges of life with resilience and hope. By prioritizing prayer and gratitude, we open ourselves to God's guidance, blessings, and favor, paving the way for sustained success and fulfillment.

As you embark on this journey of obedience, remember the importance of cultivating a lifestyle of prayer and gratitude. Seek God in prayer, express your thankfulness, and allow these practices to transform your heart and mind. By doing so, you will experience the profound impact of obedience on your life, leading you toward the success and purpose God has in store for you.

CHAPTER EIGHT

OVERCOMING ADVERSITY

L ife is a journey filled with ups and downs, and adversity is an inevitable part of that journey. Challenges and trials can arise unexpectedly, testing our strength, resilience, and faith. However, how we handle these difficult times can profoundly shape our character and determine our future success. Overcoming adversity is not only about enduring hardships, it is about learning, growing, and ultimately emerging stronger than before.

Adversity can take many forms, including personal loss, health challenges, financial struggles, relationship difficulties, and professional setbacks. While these challenges may be uncomfortable or painful, they often serve a purpose in our lives. Adversity can help us develop resilience, strengthen our faith, and deepen our understanding of ourselves and our values.

A Universal Experience

Adversity is a universal experience that affects everyone, regardless of their background or circumstances. The Bible tells us in 1 Peter 5:9, "Resist him, standing firm in the faith, because you know that the family of believers throughout the world is undergoing the same kind of sufferings." This verse reminds us that we are not alone in our struggles, others face similar challenges. Recognizing that adversity is a shared experience can provide comfort and encourage us to seek support from our community.

The Purpose of Adversity: While adversity is often uncomfortable, it serves a purpose in our lives. James 1:2-4 encourages us to "Consider it pure joy, my brothers and sisters, whenever you face trials of many kinds, because you know that the testing of your faith produces perseverance. Let perseverance finish its work so that you may be mature and complete, not lacking anything." This scripture signifies that challenges can lead to growth and maturity, shaping us into the individuals God desires us to be.

Adversity As A Teacher

Adversity often teaches us valuable lessons about ourselves, our strengths, and our faith. It challenges us to confront our weaknesses and encourages us to seek help and support. By reflecting on our experiences, we can gain insight into our values and priorities, leading to personal growth and transformation.

The Impact Of Adversity On Success

Overcoming adversity is essential for achieving long-term success. While challenges may initially seem insurmountable, they can become stepping stones to growth and achievement. Here are several ways that navigating adversity contributes to success:

Resilience Development: Resilience is the ability to bounce back from setbacks and adapt to difficult circumstances. When we face adversity, we have the opportunity to develop and strengthen our resilience. This quality is essential for success, as it enables us to persevere in the face of challenges and keep moving forward.

Character Building: Adversity often reveals our true character.

When faced with difficulties, we may discover strengths we didn't know we had. Overcoming challenges cultivates qualities such as perseverance, determination, and courage. These attributes become integral to our identity and contribute to our success in various areas of life.

Enhanced Problem-Solving Skills: Navigating adversity requires critical thinking and problem-solving skills. As we confront challenges, we learn to analyze situations, evaluate options, and develop practical solutions. This growth in problem-solving ability enhances our capacity to tackle future obstacles, making us more equipped for success.

Strengthening Relationships: Adversity can also bring people together. When we face challenges, we often turn to our support systems, friends, family, and communities, for help. These shared experiences can strengthen our relationships, creating a sense of unity and support that enhances our resilience.

Clarifying Goals and Values: Facing adversity often prompts reflection on our goals and values. During difficult times, we may reassess what is truly important to us, leading to greater clarity in our pursuits. This renewed focus helps us align our actions with our values, increasing our chances of achieving meaningful success.

Strategies For Navigating Challenges And Trials

While adversity can be daunting, there are practical strategies we can employ to navigate challenges effectively:

Maintain a Positive Mindset: Our mindset is important in how we approach adversity. Maintaining a positive outlook allows us to see challenges as opportunities for growth rather than insurmountable obstacles. Philippians 4:8 encourages us to "Think on these things: whatever is true, whatever is noble, whatever is right, whatever is pure, whatever is lovely, whatever is admirable—if anything is excellent or praiseworthy—think about such things." By focusing on the positive aspects of our situations, we can build resilience and cultivate hope.

Seek God's Guidance: In times of adversity, turning to God in prayer can provide comfort and clarity. Seek His guidance and wisdom as you navigate challenges. Psalm 32:8 assures us that God will instruct us and teach us in the way we should go. By seeking His guidance, we invite Him into our struggles and allow Him to lead us toward solutions.

Surround Yourself with Support: Don't hesitate to reach out to friends, family, or mentors for support. Sharing your struggles with trusted individuals can provide comfort and encouragement. Surrounding yourself with a supportive community allows you to draw strength from others and reminds you that you are not alone in your journey.

Set Realistic Goals: When faced with adversity, it's essential to set realistic and achievable goals. Break down larger challenges into smaller, manageable steps. This approach helps prevent overwhelm and allows you to focus on making progress one step at a time. Celebrate small victories along the way to maintain motivation.

Embrace Flexibility: Life is unpredictable, and adversity often requires us to adapt our plans. Embrace flexibility in your approach and be willing to adjust your goals or strategies as needed. Being open to change enables you to navigate challenges more effectively and find new opportunities for growth.

Reflect and Learn: After navigating a challenging experience, take time to reflect on what you have learned. Consider the lessons gained, the strengths developed, and the insights gained from the experience. Reflection allows you to grow from adversity and equips you to face future challenges with confidence.

The Power Of Faith In Adversity

For us as believers, faith is a powerful tool for overcoming adversity. Trusting in God during difficult times provides a foundation of strength and hope. Below are several ways that faith impacts our ability to navigate challenges:

Trusting God's Plan: Faith encourages us to trust in God's plan, even when we cannot see the bigger picture. Romans 8:28 reminds us that "All things work together for good to those who love God." This assurance helps us find comfort in knowing that God is in control and working for our good, even in the midst of trials.

Finding Strength in Weakness: Faith allows us to find strength in our weakness. 2 Corinthians 12:9 says, *"But He said to me, 'My grace is sufficient for you, for My power is made perfect in weakness.'"* When we acknowledge our limitations and rely on God's strength, we discover that His grace sustains us through adversity.

Experiencing Peace: Faith provides peace in the midst of turmoil. Philippians 4:7 assures us that *"the peace of God, which surpasses all understanding, will guard your hearts and minds through Christ Jesus."* This peace allows us to navigate challenges with calmness and assurance, knowing that God is with us.

Encouraging Hope: Faith instills hope, reminding us that challenges are temporary and that God has a plan for our future. Jeremiah 29:11 declares, *"For I know the plans I have for you, declares the Lord, plans to prosper you and not to harm you, plans to give you hope and a future."* This promise encourages us to hold onto hope, even in the darkest times.

Empowering Prayer: Faith fuels our prayer life. When we face adversity, prayer becomes a powerful source of strength and guidance. Through prayer, we can express our fears, seek God's wisdom, and invite Him into our struggles. God hears our prayers and is faithful to provide comfort and direction.

Learning From Biblical Examples

Throughout Scripture, we find numerous examples of individuals who faced adversity and emerged victorious through their faith and resilience. These are a few notable examples:

Job: The story of Job is a powerful testament to enduring faith in the face of unimaginable adversity. Job lost his wealth, health, and family, yet he remained steadfast in his faith. He questioned and lamented but ultimately trusted in God's sovereignty. Job's perseverance led to restoration and blessings beyond what he had before. His story serves as a reminder that even in the midst of suffering, faith can sustain us.

Joseph: Joseph faced numerous trials throughout his life, including betrayal by his brothers, slavery, and imprisonment. Yet, through it all, he remained faithful to God. Joseph's resilience and ability to see God's hand in his circumstances ultimately led him to a position of authority in Egypt, where he was able to save many lives during a famine. His journey illustrates that adversity can lead to greater purpose and impact.

David: King David experienced significant adversity, including fleeing from King Saul and facing betrayal from his son, Absalom. Despite these challenges, David continually sought God in prayer and worship. His faithfulness and reliance on God's guidance allowed him to handle difficult situations and ultimately reclaim his throne. David's life exemplifies the importance of maintaining faith and obedience, even in times of trial.

Paul: Apostle Paul faced persecution, imprisonment, and numerous hardships as he spread the Gospel. Despite the adversity he encountered, Paul remained committed to his mission. He often wrote about his struggles and emphasized rejoicing in the Lord. Philippians 4:13 reflects his unwavering faith: "*I can do all things through Christ who strengthens me.*" Paul's life demonstrates that overcoming adversity often leads to a deeper understanding of God's grace and purpose.

Adversity is an inherent part of life, but how we respond to challenges shapes our character and ultimately determines our success. We can overcome adversity and emerge stronger by navigating challenges and trials with faith, resilience, and a commitment to growth.

As you encounter challenges, remember that adversity is not the end but a catalyst for growth and transformation. Embrace the lessons learned, lean on your faith, and seek support from those around you. By building resilience and relying on God's guidance, you can navigate life's challenges with courage and grace.

In the face of adversity, remember the words of James 1:2-4: "*Consider it pure joy, my brothers and sisters, whenever you face trials of many kinds, because you know that the testing of your faith produces perseverance. Let perseverance finish its work so you may be mature and complete, not lacking anything.*" Embrace adversity as an opportunity for growth and transformation, and allow it to lead you to the success and fulfillment God has in store.

The Power Of Supernatural Lifting

Adversity is a common experience in life. However, a divine provision, supernatural liftings, exists alongside our challenges. This concept refers to the extraordinary intervention of God in our lives, enabling us to rise above our circumstances and overcome obstacles that may seem impossible.

Supernatural listings are not merely about achieving success through our efforts; they involve divine assistance that elevates us beyond our limitations. This section will explore the power of supernatural liftings, how they manifest in our lives, and the faith required to receive them.

Understanding Supernatural Liftings

Supernatural liftings are moments when God intervenes in our lives in extraordinary ways, providing us with strength, favor, and breakthroughs that we could not achieve on our own. These liftings are characterized by divine assistance, resulting in rapid progress, restoration, and elevation. They can manifest in various forms, including:

Divine Favor: Supernatural liftings often come in the form of divine favor, where God opens previously closed doors and grants us opportunities that seem beyond our reach. This favor can lead to unexpected promotions, financial blessings, and connections with influential people who support our endeavors.

Miraculous Healing: In physical or emotional distress, supernatural liftings may manifest as miraculous healing. When we turn to God in faith, He can restore our health and well-being, lifting us from despair and empowering us to continue our journey.

Restoration and Reconciliation: Supernatural liftings can also involve restoring relationships, dreams, and opportunities that may have been lost due to adversity. God can mend broken relationships and restore areas of our lives beyond repair.

Transformative Breakthroughs: These liftings can lead to breakthroughs in various aspects of life, whether in our careers, finances, or personal goals. They are moments when God intervenes in ways that transform our circumstances, allowing us to experience progress and success that surpasses our efforts.

Biblical Examples Of Supernatural Lifting

The Bible is filled with accounts of individuals who experienced supernatural lifting. These stories are powerful reminders of God's ability to elevate and transform those who trust Him.

Joseph: The story of Joseph is a profound example of supernatural liftings. Joseph faced incredible adversity, including betrayal by his brothers, slavery, and imprisonment. However, despite these challenges, God's favor was upon him. In Genesis 41, God elevated

Joseph from the prison to the palace, making him second in command in Egypt. This supernatural lifting restored Joseph's fortunes and enabled him to save countless lives during a famine. Joseph's journey illustrates that God can intervene and lift us to new heights, even in the darkest moments.

Esther: Esther's story is another powerful example of divine intervention and favor. As a Jewish woman in a foreign land, Esther faced the threat of destruction along with her people. However, through her courage and faith, she approached King Xerxes and pleaded for her people. God granted her favor, and she was able to save the Jewish nation from destruction. Esther's elevation from an orphaned girl to a queen demonstrates how God can use individuals to effect supernatural liftings for His purpose.

David: a shepherd boy, David faced numerous adversities before becoming king. He was pursued by King Saul and had to navigate challenges that tested his faith and character. Despite these trials, David remained faithful to God. Ultimately, God lifted David from obscurity to the throne of Israel, fulfilling the promise made to him. David's story reminds us that God sees our struggles and can elevate us to fulfill our divine purpose.

The Early Church: In the New Testament, we see the early church experiencing supernatural liftings through the power of the Holy Spirit. Acts 2 recounts the day of Pentecost when the Holy Spirit descended upon the disciples, empowering them to preach the Gospel boldly. This supernatural lifting resulted in thousands coming to faith and the early church's rapid growth. The empowerment of the Holy Spirit is a reminder that God can elevate His people to accomplish great things for His Kingdom.

The Conditions For Supernatural Liftings

While supernatural liftings demonstrate God's grace and favor, some conditions can help us position ourselves to receive them. These conditions include:

Faith: Faith is the foundation for experiencing supernatural liftings. Hebrews 11:6 reminds us that *"without faith, it is impossible to please Him."* When we approach God with faith, believing He can intervene in our lives, we open ourselves to His divine assistance. Our faith enables us to trust His timing and guidance, even when circumstances seem challenging.

Obedience: Living a life of obedience to God's commands positions us to receive His favor. When we align our actions with His will, we demonstrate our commitment. John 14:21 emphasizes this connection: *"He who has My commandments and keeps them, it is he who loves Me. And he who loves Me will be loved by My Father, and I will love him and manifest Myself to him."* Obedience opens the door for God's presence and favor in our lives.

Prayer and Seeking God: Regular prayer and seeking God's presence are essential for inviting supernatural liftings into our lives. When we develop a lifestyle of prayer, we align our hearts with God's purposes and open ourselves to His guidance. James 4:8 encourages us to *"draw near to God, and He will draw near to you."* This promise underscores the importance of prayerfully seeking God, allowing us to experience His presence and intervention.

Gratitude: A gratitude attitude positions us to receive God's blessings. When we express thankfulness for what we have, we acknowledge God's goodness and faithfulness. Gratitude opens our hearts to receive more from God. 1 Thessalonians 5:18 instructs us to *"give thanks in all circumstances; for this is the will of God in Christ Jesus for you."* By practicing gratitude, we invite God's favor into our lives,

Humility: Humility is a crucial condition for experiencing supernatural liftings. When we approach God humbly, acknowledging our dependence on Him, we create a posture inviting His intervention. James 4:10 reminds us, *"Humble yourselves before the Lord, and He will exalt you."* Humility positions us to receive God's grace and favor in our lives.

Embracing The Process Of Overcoming Adversity

While supernatural liftings can lead to rapid breakthroughs and successes, it is essential to remember that overcoming adversity often involves a process. This process can be challenging, requiring patience, perseverance, and faith. Here are some practical steps to embrace the journey of overcoming adversity:

Acknowledge the Challenge: The first step in overcoming adversity is acknowledging our challenges. Denying or minimizing our struggles does not lead to growth; instead, it hinders our ability to seek solutions. By accepting our circumstances, we can better assess the situation and develop a plan for moving forward.

Seek God's Wisdom: When faced with adversity, turn to God for wisdom and guidance. Pray for clarity and understanding, asking Him to show you the way forward. Proverbs 2:6 affirms, *"For the Lord gives wisdom; from His mouth come knowledge and understanding."* Trust that God will provide the insight you need to navigate challenges effectively.

Develop Resilience: Resilience is the ability to bounce back from setbacks and adapt to challenges. Cultivating resilience involves developing a positive mindset, maintaining hope, and embracing change. When faced with difficulties, focus on the lessons learned and the growth opportunities that arise from the experience.

Take Action: Overcoming adversity requires proactive steps. Identify practical actions you can take to address the challenges you face. Whether seeking help, developing new skills, or adjusting your plans, taking action empowers you to regain control and progress toward your goals.

Maintain Community Support: Lean on your support system during challenging times. Share your struggles with trusted friends, family, or mentors who can offer encouragement and guidance. Community support provides strength and reassurance, reminding us we are not alone.

Practice Gratitude During Trials: Intentionally practice gratitude during adversity. Acknowledge the blessings you still have and the lessons you learned through challenges. Focusing on gratitude shifts your perspective and helps you find hope even in difficult circumstances.

Trust God's Timing: Overcoming adversity often involves waiting on God's timing. Trust that He works behind the scenes, even when you cannot see the outcome. Ecclesiastes 3:11 reminds us, *"He has made everything beautiful in its time."* Patience and trust allow you to embrace the process, knowing God's perfect timing.

The Role Of Faith In Supernatural Liftings

Faith is the catalyst for experiencing supernatural liftings in our lives. When we trust God, we invite His divine intervention and favor. Let's see some critical aspects of faith that enhance our ability to receive supernatural liftings:

Expectancy: Faith involves a sense of expectancy, believing God can intervene in our lives. Hebrews 11:1 defines faith as *"the substance of things hoped for, the evidence of things not seen."* Expecting God's intervention opens our hearts to receive His blessings and align our actions with His promises.

Perseverance: Faith requires perseverance, especially during challenging times. When faced with adversity, it can be tempting to lose hope. However, Romans 5:3-4 reminds us that *"we also glory in tribulations, knowing that tribulation produces perseverance; perseverance, character; and character, hope."* By persevering in faith, we strengthen our character and deepen our trust in God's plan.

Prayerful Faith: Faith and prayer are interconnected. Prayer expresses our faith, allowing us to communicate with God and seek His guidance. In Mark 11:24, Jesus teaches us the power of faith in prayer: "*Therefore I say to you, whatever things you ask when you pray, believe that you receive them, and you will have them.*" We approach God in prayer with faith and position ourselves to receive His supernatural liftings.

Faith in God's Promises: Holding onto God's promises is essential for navigating adversity. Scripture is filled with promises of God's faithfulness, provision, and protection. When we anchor our faith in His promises, we gain the confidence to face challenges with hope. Psalm 119:105 reminds us, "*Your word is a lamp to my feet and a light to my path.*" God's promises illuminate our path, guiding us through adversity.

Community of Faith: Surrounding ourselves with a community of believers strengthens our faith during challenging times. Fellowship with other believers provides encouragement, support, and shared testimonies of God's faithfulness. Hebrews 10:24-25 urges us to "*consider one another to stir up love and good works, not forsaking the assembling of ourselves together.*" Being part of a community of faith reinforces our trust in God's power to lift us in times of adversity.

Finally, overcoming adversity through supernatural liftings is a testament to God's grace and power. By embracing our challenges with faith, resilience, and a willingness to seek God's guidance, we open ourselves up to divine intervention that elevates us above our circumstances.

As you navigate the adversities in your life, remember the power of supernatural liftings. Trust in God's promises, embrace a lifestyle of prayer and gratitude and maintain a spirit of expectancy. Embrace the journey, knowing each challenge is an opportunity for growth and transformation.

Through supernatural liftings, you can rise above adversity and experience the blessings and favor that come from living in obedience to God. Allow Him to lift you and guide you toward the success and fulfillment He has in store.

Turning Trials Into Triumphs

Turning trials into triumphs requires a shift in perspective, a commitment to personal growth, and a reliance on faith and resilience. Trials are an inevitable part of the human experience. They come in various forms, such as health challenges, financial difficulties, relationship struggles, loss, or career setbacks.

While trials can be painful and disheartening, they also serve as catalysts for growth and transformation. How we respond to these challenges can significantly influence our journey toward success.

Understanding the Purpose of Trials: Trials often serve a higher purpose. James 1:2-4 reminds us, *"Consider it pure joy, my brothers and sisters, whenever you face trials of many kinds, because you know that testing your faith produces perseverance. Let perseverance finish its work so you may be mature and complete, not lacking anything."*

The Reality of Suffering: Suffering is a universal experience that connects us as human beings. The Bible does not shy away from depicting the struggles of its characters. For instance, Job endured immense suffering, yet he emerged with a deeper understanding of God's sovereignty and faithfulness. Recognizing that suffering is a shared experience can help us feel less isolated during difficult times.

Finding Meaning in Trials: Every trial has the potential for learning and growth. When faced with adversity, ask yourself: "What can I learn from this experience?" Reflecting on the lessons gained can shift your perspective and help you see the trial as an opportunity for development. Trials challenge us to examine our beliefs, priorities, and values, leading to greater self-awareness.

Shifting Perspective: From Trials to Triumphs
Transforming trials into triumphs begins with a shift in perspective. Instead of viewing challenges as insurmountable

obstacles, we can see them as opportunities for growth and transformation. This mindset shift is crucial for navigating adversity with resilience.

Embracing a Growth Mindset: A growth mindset believes that hard work and perseverance can develop our abilities and intelligence. When we adopt a growth mindset, we view challenges as opportunities to learn and grow. Instead of fearing failure, we embrace it as a stepping stone toward success. Philippians 4:13 reminds us, "*I can do all things through Christ who strengthens me.*" This assurance empowers us to face trials with confidence.

Focusing on Solutions: During challenging times, it is easy to become consumed by negativity and despair. However, shifting focus from the problem to potential solutions can help us navigate adversity more effectively. Instead of dwelling on what is wrong, ask yourself, "*What can I do to improve this situation?*" This proactive approach fosters a sense of empowerment and encourages us to take constructive action.

Seeking Support and Encouragement: Turning trials into triumphs often requires support from others. Contact trusted friends, family, or mentors who can encourage and guide you. Surrounding yourself with a supportive community fosters resilience and reminds you that you are not alone in your struggles.

Cultivating Resilience: Resilience is the ability to bounce back from setbacks and adapt to challenges. It is a crucial quality for turning trials into triumphs. Building resilience involves developing coping strategies, maintaining a positive outlook, and adapting to changing circumstances. Romans 5:3-4 encourages us to say, "We *also glory in tribulations, knowing that tribulation produces perseverance; perseverance, character; and character, hope.*" Embracing resilience allows us to view trials as opportunities for growth and development.

Learning From Trials

Trials offer valuable lessons that can shape our character and equip us for future challenges. Reflecting on the lessons learned and how they can contribute to our personal growth is essential as we go through adversity.

Gaining Strength: Trials often reveal our inner strength and resilience. When faced with challenges, we may discover abilities and qualities we did not know we possessed. Reflecting on past trials allows us to acknowledge our growth and recognize that we can overcome difficulties. This newfound strength empowers us to face future challenges with confidence.

Developing Empathy: Experiencing trials can foster empathy and compassion for others facing similar challenges. Our struggles enable us to connect with others on a deeper level, allowing us to offer support and encouragement. 2 Corinthians 1:4 reminds us that God comforts us in our troubles so that we can comfort others. Our experiences can be a source of strength and inspiration for those around us.

Strengthening Faith: Trials often lead us to a deeper reliance on God. When we face challenges beyond our control, we are prompted to seek His guidance and strength. Our faith is tested and refined, allowing us to experience God's faithfulness profoundly. Romans 8:28 assures us that "*all things work together for good to those who love God.*" Trusting in this promise during trials strengthens our faith and deepens our relationship with God.

Redefining Success: Adversity can lead us to redefine our understanding of success. When we face challenges, we may realize that true success is not solely about achieving external goals but also about personal growth, resilience, and character development. This shift in perspective allows us to celebrate our progress and achievements, even in the face of adversity.

Turning Trials Into Triumphs Through Faith

Faith is a powerful tool for transforming trials into triumphs. When we trust God, we open ourselves to His guidance, strength, and supernatural intervention. Here are some key aspects of faith that help us navigate adversity:

Trusting God's Promises: Holding onto God's promises is essential during trials. Scripture is filled with assurances of His faithfulness, provision, and guidance. When we remind ourselves of God's promises, we cultivate hope and confidence in His ability to see us through challenging times. Psalm 119:50 states, *"This is my comfort in my affliction, for Your word has given me life."* Meditating on God's promises nourishes our faith and strengthens our resolve.

Praying with Expectancy: Prayer is vital to turning trials into triumphs. When we pray with expectancy, we invite God into our circumstances and trust Him to intervene. Philippians 4:6-7 encourages us to pray to God, promising that His peace will guard our hearts and minds. Expecting God to move in our situations fosters hope and resilience.

Embracing God's Strength: Our strength is limited, but God's strength is limitless. When we rely on His strength, we can face challenges with confidence. Isaiah 40:31 assures us that *"those who hope in the Lord will renew their strength."* By embracing God's strength, we empower ourselves to overcome obstacles and transform trials into triumphs.

Finding Purpose in Trials: Faith helps us find purpose in our trials. Rather than viewing challenges as setbacks, we can see them as opportunities for growth and learning. God can use our experiences to fulfill His purpose in our lives and help us become vessels for His glory. Romans 5:3-4 emphasizes that our sufferings produce perseverance, character, and hope, illustrating how adversity can lead to a greater purpose.

Worshiping in the Storm: Worship is a powerful expression of faith, especially during trials. When we worship God amid difficulties, we trust Him and acknowledge His sovereignty. Worship shifts our focus from our problems to God's greatness, providing strength and encouragement. Acts 16:25-26 recounts the story of Paul and Silas, who worshiped in prison, leading to miraculous deliverance. Worship has the power to transform our circumstances and elevate our spirits.

Turning trials into triumphs is a powerful journey that requires faith, resilience, and a willingness to grow. Adversity can catalyze transformation, allowing us to develop character, strength, and a deeper understanding of God's faithfulness.

As you face challenges in your life, remember that trials do not define you; instead, they provide opportunities for growth and triumph. Embrace the lessons learned, lean on your faith, and seek support from those around you. By adopting a perspective of growth and resilience, you can turn your trials into triumphs and experience the abundant life God has in store for you.

Through faith and perseverance, you can emerge from adversity stronger, wiser, and more equipped to fulfill your purpose. Embrace the journey, knowing that God is with you every step of the way, ready to lift you and lead you to triumph over every trial.

CONCLUSION

Reflecting On Your Journey

As we reach the end of this book, we must recognize that each of us has a unique story to tell. Life's challenges are integral to our journey, shaping our character, deepening our faith, and ultimately leading us toward fulfilling our purpose.

Embracing your success story involves acknowledging both the trials and triumphs you have achieved along the way. Every challenge you have encountered has contributed to your growth and development.

Your trials have tested your resolve and resilience, while your triumphs have illuminated the path forward. Each step of your journey is significant and worth celebrating.

Embracing your success story means recognizing that you are not defined solely by your accomplishments or failures but by the journey itself, the lessons learned, the strength gained, and the faith developed.

Take time to reflect on the experiences that have shaped your life. Consider the challenges you have faced and how you have overcome them.

Acknowledge the moments of growth and transformation that

have brought you to where you are today. This reflection is a way to celebrate your successes and remind you of your resilience and capacity to overcome adversity.

Share Your Story
Your story has the power to inspire others.
You can encourage those facing similar challenges by sharing your experiences, both the struggles and the victories.

Your journey can symbolize hope, demonstrating that it is possible to turn trials into triumphs.
Consider writing, speaking, or engaging in conversations that allow you to share your story and inspire others to embrace their paths to success.

Recognize Your Growth
Embracing your success story involves recognizing the growth from your experiences.
Every trial has equipped you with valuable skills, insights, and strengths to serve you in the future.
Acknowledge the lessons learned and how they have shaped your perspective. This recognition empowers you to approach future challenges with confidence and resilience.

Developing a Mindset of Gratitude
Gratitude is a powerful tool for embracing your success story. Focusing on the blessings in your life and the lessons learned through adversity can help you develop a positive mindset that enhances your overall well-being.

Gratitude shifts your focus from what you lack to what you have, allowing you to appreciate the journey and celebrate your achievements.

Final Thoughts and Encouragement
As you reflect on your journey and embrace your success story, remember that overcoming adversity is not a destination but a continuous process.

Life will present new challenges, but with each challenge comes the opportunity for growth, resilience, and transformation. Your past experiences have equipped you to face whatever lies ahead with confidence and faith.

Stay committed to growth and learning.

Seek opportunities to develop your skills, expand your knowledge, and deepen your understanding of yourself and your purpose.

Trust in God's Plan

Maintain your trust in God's plan for your life.

His promises are steadfast, and He is faithful to guide you through every season.

As Jeremiah 29:11 reminds us, *"For I know the plans I have for you, declares the Lord, plans to prosper you and not to harm you, plans to give you hope and a future."* (Jeremiah 29:11, NIV)

Trusting in His plan allows you to approach life's challenges confidently, knowing that He is working all things together for your good.

Celebrate Your Victories

Take time to celebrate your victories, both big and small. Acknowledge your achievements and the progress you have made along the way. Celebrating your victories reinforces your sense of accomplishment and motivates you to strive for success.

Encourage Others

As you embrace your success story, be a source of encouragement to others.

Share your insights, offer support, and inspire those around you to pursue their dreams.

Your journey can testify to the power of faith, resilience, and hard work.

Finally, embracing your success story means recognizing that your journey, filled with trials and triumphs, is a testament to your resilience, faith, and commitment to growth.

As you face the challenges ahead, remember that you have the strength and capacity to turn trials into triumphs.

Your success story is unfolding, and with each step you take, you are writing a narrative of hope, transformation, and achievement.

A SPECIAL CALL TO SALVATION & NEW BEGINNINGS FROM APOSTLE DR. DAVID PHILEMON

Dear Beloved,

God loves you deeply and has brought you to this moment for a reason. No matter your past, His love and forgiveness are available to you.

The Bible says in John 3:16, "For God so loved the world that He gave His one and only Son, that whoever believes in Him shall not perish but have eternal life." Jesus Christ came to save you, offering you a new life of purpose and peace.

If you're ready to accept Jesus as your Lord and Savior, pray this simple prayer:

The Salvation Prayer

"Heavenly Father, I come to You in the Name of Jesus. I acknowledge that I am a sinner in need of a Savior. I believe that Jesus Christ is Your Son, that He died for my sins, and that You raised Him from the dead. I repent of my sins and turn to You with

my
Whole heart. Jesus, I ask You to come into my life. Be my Lord and my Savior. I surrender my life to You. Fill me with Your Holy Spirit, guide me on the path of righteousness, and help me to follow Your script for my life. Thank you, Father, for saving me. In the name of Jesus. Amen."

Welcome to the Family of God!

If you have just prayed this prayer, Congratulations! You are now a child of God, and heaven is rejoicing. Your journey has begun, and we're here to support you as you grow in faith and discover God's unique plans for you.

Next Steps:
• Connect with a Bible-believing church.
• Read the Bible Daily: God's Word is your guide.
• Pray Regularly: Prayer is your lifeline to God.
• Share Your Faith: Don't keep the good news to yourself.

www.ingramcontent.com/pod-product-compliance
Lightning Source LLC
Chambersburg PA
CBHW071859020426
42331CB00010B/2592